Roger Evans was born in Bridgwater in 1947, the son of Bill and Dot Evans, and has one sister, Pat, who has illustrated a number of his earlier publications. He was educated in Bridgwater at Dr. Morgan's Grammar School for Boys and now serves as secretary to the old boys' association.

An early interest in his home town and county resulted in him becoming the youngest ever councillor to serve on the Bridgwater Borough Council. From his childhood, he has had an active interest in the local carnival scene, being a founder member of a Bridgwater Carnival Club, a former chairman for Bridgwater Carnival and now serves as a senior judge.

After thirty three years in industry as an IT specialist, he turned to lecturing and authoring, and has published several books on Bridgwater and Somerset including *Blame it on the Cider, Somerset Stories of the Supernatural* and *Landscapes of Somerset*. He now works for Bridgwater College and the Somerset carnival community, developing courses in the performance arts, craft skills, event stewarding and other carnival related subjects.

Well known across the county as a story teller and raconteur, fifty-seven-year-old Roger has been married to Lorna for thirty five years. They have four children and four grandchildren, all living in Somerset. A keen walker, in between his college activities and writing, he spends his spare time walking the county, mostly in his much loved Quantock Hills, where he can regularly be found with his Border Collie at heel.

SOMERSET'S
Forgotten Heroes

ROGER EVANS

THE DOVECOTE PRESS

First published in 2004 by
The Dovecote Press Ltd
Stanbridge, Wimborne, Dorset BH21 4JD

ISBN 1 904349 32 3

Printed and bound by The Baskerville Press Ltd, Salisbury, Wiltshire

All papers used by The Dovecote Press are natural, recyclable products
made from wood grown in sustainable, well-managed forests.

A CIP catalogue record for this book is available
from the British Library

Contents

Introduction 6

Sarah Biffen 8

More Heroines 16

Defending the Empire 27

World Wars 48

The Cruel Sea 67

Rescues 82

For the Greater Good 100

Introduction

Heroes are distinguished by their courage. Unfortunately, most are soon quickly forgotten. I remember the early days of television when programmes such as 'This is Your Life' sang the praises of unsung heroes like a Glasgow fireman, a Norfolk lifeboatman, a nurse who was first on the scene of a major disaster. Today the programme is full of celebrities from TV soaps and, for me, has lost its direction.

In the pages that follow, I try to recapture that spirit of remembering our true heroes. This book tells the story of more than eighty Somerset folk who I have singled out for their exceptional courage or outstanding qualities. These not only include twenty four Victoria Crosses and twenty one other awards for bravery, but a complete cross-section of ordinary men and women whose courage or heroism should never be forgotten.

Sarah Biffen was born with no arms and no legs. And yet, having been sold by her parents to a travelling freak show, she overcame her disabilities and rose to eminence as a portrait painter. Frances Barkley was the first European woman to set foot on Hawaii and British Columbia, as well as the first woman to twice circumnavigate the world. Margaret Bondfield became the nation's first cabinet minister.

Somerset men were at the Battle of Trafalgar, in the Charge of the Light Brigade, at Rorke's Drift and the Bridge on the River Kwai. For these, their moments of glory came in the field of battle, but at home others showed equal courage during the Baedeker raids on Bath, at mining disasters in north Somerset and in lifeboat rescues along the Somerset coastline. Francis Foley demonstrated his outstanding courage performing an office job in Berlin, whilst at the same time helping more than 10,000 Jews to escape the Holocaust.

In 1995 I was shown a headstone in my local cemetery on which was inscribed, 'Erected by friends to commemorate one of the gallant six hundred'. Could this be a memorial to one of the few survivors of the Charge of the Light Brigade? I investigated and discovered the story of Denis Heron, a story of outstanding courage. And yet, here in the corner

6

of the cemetery, the cross over his grave was leaning forward at such an angle that, with the passing of one or two more winters, it would have fallen and the inscription would have been lost forever. I was determined he should not be forgotten and his story was my inspiration for this book.

I would like to thank the following for their help in providing the illustrations: Robin Bush (Sarah Biffen), Jake Simpson (Mary Ann Rogers), Chard Town Council (Margaret Bondfield), King's Own Royal Border Regiment Museum (Major Frederick Elton), 12th Regiment Royal Artillery (George Renny), Army Medical Services Museum, Aldershot (John Crimmin & Sir Neville Reginald Howse), The South Wales Borderers and Monmouthshire Regimental Museum of the Royal Regiment of Wales (Lt. John Rouse Merriott Chard and Campbell Mellis Douglas), Martin Hornby, WFA Liaison Trustee (Rev. Edward Mellish), Royal Welch Fusiliers Regimental Museum (John Collins), Michael Smith (Francis Foley) from *Foley: The Spy Who Saved 10,000 Jews* by Michael Smith (new edition Oct 2004 Politicos), Bath & NE Somerset Library Service (Regina Hotel, Bath), Royal Hampshire Regiment Museum (Herbert Wallace Le Patourel), Rod Authers (Ron Authers), Imperial War Museum (Gerard Roope & Wilfred Fuller), Roderick and Eleanor Dixon (Captain George Lewis Browne), Radstock Museum (Lower Conygre Mine, Timsbury), Somerset Archaeological and Natural History Society (Exmoor Blizzards), Paul Stubbles (Paul Stubbles & Paul Williams), Chard Museum (Daisy and John Stringfellow), Andy Elson (Andy Elson and Colin Prescott), Associated Sports (Mary Rand). I would also like to thank Pat Frost for the drawings of Sarah Biffen and Denis Heron.

At times, when working on this book , and pondering on how soon we forget our heroes, lines from Ralph McTell's song 'Streets of London' have passed through my thoughts.

> *And have you seen the old man outside the seaman's mission,*
> *His memory fading with those ribbons that he wears*
> *And in our winter city, the rain cries a little pity*
> *For one more forgotten hero, and a world that doesn't care.*

I cared enough to write this book, and I thank you, the reader, for caring enough to wish to share with me the stories of the heroes I have discovered.

ROGER EVANS, Bridgwater
October 2004

ONE

Sarah Biffen

'Show me a hero and I will write you a tragedy'. These words of F. Scott Fitzgerald are especially true when applied to Sarah Biffen. Hers was a 'rags to riches – and back' story worthy of the best of Dickens. Sarah was born into a farm labouring family without the benefit of arms, hands, feet or legs. And yet, through her own endeavours and fortitude, she became an artist of the highest standing, patronised by no fewer than four British kings and queens, the King of Holland and a string of dukes, duchesses and other worthies from her time. Her life was a catalogue of drama and tragedy, and yet this incredible lady's story has remained largely untold.

Humble beginnings

Sarah Biffen was one of five children. Her father, Henry, was a farm labourer and shoe maker in the village of East Quantoxhead on the Somerset coast. Aged twenty four, he had married Sarah Perkins in the picturesque village church. The following year their first born arrived, a son named John who died in infancy, but in the years that followed four more children were born, the third of these being Sarah, on 25 October 1784, and the heroine of our story.

It must have been devastating for her parents to see her born limbless. These were hard times in which to survive with such disabilities. It was not uncommon for a child with severe handicaps to be put to one side, allowed to 'slip away'. But Sarah's parents were of tougher stock and accepted their responsibilities, no doubt tempered with concerns for their child's future.

Sarah suffered from what today would be called phocomelia, a condition believed to be linked to cottage industries such as blanket-making, which used toxic dyes. Today we associate this condition with the drug known as Thalidomide.

Childhood

Sarah had stumps on her shoulders where the arms should have been. She had no legs, only simply rudimentary toes at the base of her body. It is difficult to imagine how her parents coped with three other children and the long hours of the rural working classes in an age when holidays were few.

As her brother and sisters grew, exploring the wooded coombes of the neighbouring Quantock Hills or the windswept Bristol Channel coast, Sarah could only watch. We know that as an eight year old she had expressed the desire to be taught how to use needle and cotton to make her own clothes. How she achieved those skills defies belief, but acquire them she did, for in her brief autobiographical notes (*An Interesting Narrative, 1821*) she wrote:

'At the age of eight I was very desirous of acquiring the use of my needle; but my parents discouraged the idea, thinking it wholly impracticable. I was not, however, intimidated, and whenever my father and mother were absent, I was continually practising every invention, till at length I could, with my mouth – thread a needle – tie a knot – do fancy work – cut out and make my own dresses.

At the age of twelve my desire to work with the needle having worked so far, gave place to my inclination to write: and in a short time I was enabled to correspond with distant friends.'

Oddly these were skills associated with the landed gentry rather than the family of an agricultural labourer.

Sarah's determination, perhaps bordering on stubbornness, is also reflected in an account of her Sunday visits to the local church, where she refused offers of help to carry her down the aisle to where her family sat. Instead she would roll down until she reached the required row of pews and then somehow bounce herself into her seat.

Sarah's future

Sarah's future was a great concern to her parents. They knew they would not always be able to look after her and a solution had to be found through which Sarah could gain her independence. She was approaching her teenage years. It was not a case of wanting to get rid of her, simply to secure her future well being. What happened next is speculation on my part, but I believe is the most probable account of this undocumented period.

It was the last Wednesday in September, St. Mathew's Day, and the day of Bridgwater Fair, a hiring fair at which servants and labourers hired themselves out for the following year. It was also an occasion to buy and sell sheep and ponies, and all those household items that needed to be bought when much of a family's shopping was done but once a year. So large was the gathering that it was a major attraction for all sorts of thieves, rogues and vagabonds. It was also a fair with its share of side shows, strong men, bearded ladies, freak animals and other crowd-pulling abnormalities. An armless, legless lady, lacking hands yet able to thread a needle and make her own clothes would have been a real fairground attraction, a scoop to an agent with an eye to turn an opportunity into profit.

Sold at the Fair

Sarah's parents annually made the 14 mile journey from East Quantoxhead to Bridgwater for the fair. There they found Mr. Emmanuel Dukes with a travelling side show, a friendly enough character who appeared to be honest. Perhaps he had a role for Sarah, now aged thirteen, and could provide her with the opportunity to win her independence and achieve financial security through her endeavours. Dukes could give her the chance to travel the country, to visit places and meet people in a way that was impossible whilst living at home. She could already cut, sew and write by mouth. What an attraction she might prove to be.

Would her parents have received payment for such a transaction? Almost certainly, for that was the way of the world in the eighteenth century. And so it was that at Bridgwater Fair in 1797 or 1798, Sarah said goodbye to her family and joined the entourage of Mr. Emmanuel Dukes.

And here the speculation ends, for we know that she was bound to Mr. Dukes by written contract and thereafter travelled the country with him, exhibiting her amazing talents. It was a transaction of which she once wrote, 'Shortly after this it was suggested to my parents that a comfortable living might be obtained by public exhibition, and an engagement was arranged for that purpose; but the result was by no means equal to the expectations raised, and fourteen years of my life thus passed away without any substantial benefits to me'.

The earliest record of her appearances comes from a Thomas Rowlandson cartoon of St. Bartholomew's Fair in 1799 at Smithfield in which a van is depicted with a poster on one side referring to the limbless lady carrying the title of 'Miss Biffen'. And so Sarah was destined to join the world of the travelling caravans and life on the highway.

The Eighth Wonder of the World

Sarah spent the following fourteen years travelling the fairgrounds with Mr. Dukes. Posters declared that '(what) renders her worthy of notice, is the industrious and astonishing means she has invented and practised to obtain the use of the needle, scissors, pens, pencils, etc. wherein she is extremely adroit: she can cut out and make any part of her own clothes, sews extremely neat and in a most wonderful manner: writes well, she has practised the art of drawing 16 months, and miniature painting only 5 months, wherein she astonishes even eminent artists, all of which she performs principally with her mouth.'

At the age of twenty, Sarah was a fully grown woman, and yet she never grew to more than thirty seven inches tall. Despite her lack of height, she was always 'aspiring to further acquirements' and 'felt anxious to try my skill in the art of painting'. So after some six years with little change to her act, Dukes took it upon himself to teach her painting. A year later, she was producing miniatures to such a high standard that she earned herself the billing of the 'Eighth Wonder of the World'.

George Long witnessed Sarah at work when she was forty four years old, and described how 'this lady's ability was indeed unique, as she had neither arms nor legs, being born with only short stumps of both. Her appearance is handsome, as seemingly seated on a cushion she deftly plied her needle with her mouth, with which too she threaded it, her work resting on her shoulder stump. She worked both in plain sewing and embroidery, but she also painted miniature portraits, handed round for inspection, and she wrote her name, in an excellent lady's handwriting as we should call it but executed, as all else, by her mouth alone'.

Sarah, whilst tied to Mr. Dukes, travelled the country and was viewed by all and sundry. Her income was £5 per year and she lived as one of the family. The public paid one shilling for a seat in the pits or sixpence in the gallery to see her perform. As an additional source of income, she painted miniatures on ivory at a cost of three guineas, the proceeds accruing to Mr. Dukes who promised 5,000 guineas to anyone who could prove his act was a fraud.

The Earl of Morton and royal patronage

On one such occasion, at St. Bartholomew's Fair, she was watched by the Earl of Morton. He observed her complete a portrait, but not the whole process. He was somewhat suspicious and agreed to sit for a portrait of his own. It must have taken a considerable time and a number of sittings, for we know that, in order to ensure her integrity, he took the unfinished portrait away at the end of each of them.

The completed work was taken to King George IIII. So impressed was his majesty that he agreed to fund lessons for Sarah from William Craig, himself a painter in watercolours to the Queen, and miniature painter to the Duke and Duchess of York and the Duke of Kent. Her ability moved forward in leaps and bounds. With her paint brush in her mouth and the handle end of the brush passed through a loop on her shoulder, she created miniatures, as small as two and a half inches across, of the highest standard. And yet despite her talent and the patronage of increasingly influential benefactors, she remained on the fairgrounds.

The Earl of Morton was eager to release Sarah from the freak show life to which she was subjected, but Sarah was determined to honour her contract with Mr. Dukes, who she considered to have always shown her nothing but kindness.

Reluctance to leave the fairgrounds

To some extent we can understand her reluctance to leave. She came from humble beginnings and faced an uncertain future. Accepted into the family of Mr. Dukes, she had spent more than half her life with him and no doubt had developed a stronger feeling of security than during those days at East Quantoxhead. To abandon a comfortable routine, and a secure roof over her head, was no doubt a daunting prospect.

Her travels continued; London, Norwich, Oxford, Exeter, Plymouth, Swansea and Cheltenham. The list goes on. But in 1816 the *Cheltenham Chronicle* makes reference to her residence in the town and it appears she had finally been persuaded to settle down. No further references to her fairground activities can be found beyond that of Swansea in 1815. It appears the Earl of Morton's persuasion had triumphed, for in 1819 Sarah had her own residence in London and a studio on the Strand. Her clientele was expanding. Two years later, the Earl of Morton took Sarah to Brussels where she was introduced to the Prince of Orange, who appointed her to the position of miniaturist to the King of Holland. Sarah had truly arrived.

It is perhaps tempting to imagine that charity motivated Sarah's patrons, but that would belittle her true capabilities. Her work was now of such a high standard that in the same year as her visit to Brussels, the Royal Society of Arts presented her with their Silver Award, a recognition not lightly given. And in announcing the award, the Society's president, the Duke of Sussex, appealed to the membership to offer their patronage and comfort to Sarah. Meanwhile Sarah stayed in Brussels painting for the Dutch court until 1822. This daughter of a Somerset agricultural labourer had joined the roll call of internationally recognised artists.

Betrayed

Life was about to deal Sarah a most cruel blow. Sarah, now approaching forty, fell in love with William Wright, a Londoner and a banker's clerk, who she married in September 1824. Could this have been a marriage of convenience with some other purpose? Certainly not on Sarah's part, for Sarah and William travelled all the way to her home just outside Bridgwater to be married at the hamlet church at Kilton, near Kilve. This surely confirms Sarah's wish to be wed in the traditional manner, and shows her love for William. If Sarah's intentions were honourable – the same cannot be said for those of her husband.

William Wright persuaded Sarah that he was better fitted than her to look after her financial affairs. Her accumulated wealth, no doubt intended to see her through her later years, was given into his keeping. Within weeks of gaining control of her purse strings, he left. For a while he granted her just £40 per year from what previously had been her own money. But this was short-lived and she was left impoverished, just able to pay her way as long as she remained able to work.

The loss of her benefactor

Throughout this difficult period, the Earl of Morton continued to keep in touch by writing, indeed right up to his death in 1827. With his passing went perhaps her greatest benefactor and guardian. Who else, throughout her life, with the exception of her parents, had shown such a selfless interest in her welfare?

She had lost her husband, her wealth and her benefactor. There appeared to be no alternative but to return to the life of travelling the fairgrounds, but now as an independent artist responsible for her own publicity. To her embarrassment she was also obliged to appeal to former patrons for financial support. As a result of this appeal, endorsed by Princess Augusta, Sarah received a pension from the Civil List of £12 per year.

Tragedies

Further personal tragedies were to follow with the death of her eighty-seven-year-old father in 1835 and her mother the following year, aged ninety three. Both remain at rest in the village of East Quantoxhead. Shortly afterwards, Sarah's most supportive royal patron, Princess Augusta, also died.

In 1837 she was living in Brighton and painting likenesses of royalty copied from the works of others. By 1841 she had returned to Cheltenham and was clearly considering embarking on a new life in America. But it was in Liverpool that she was to arrive before the year was out, and there she remained for the rest of her life.

She set up a studio in Bold Street and attracted a reasonable clientele, at least to begin with. Ill health took its toll and her income as an artist waned, and with it her ability to maintain a reasonable quality of life. She was on a cruel and unstoppable downward spiral, moving from lodging to lodging, each of a lesser standard, reflecting her own decline.

In 1847, Richard Rathbone launched an appeal to raise funds for this remarkable lady, now unable to maintain the dignity for which she once fought for so hard. The royal family and various celebrities contributed and her lot was temporarily eased.

She was tormented in her final days by a long illness which caused great difficulty in breathing. In October 1850, at the age of 66 her suffering came to an end. She died in poverty at her lodgings at 8 Duke

Street in Liverpool. The inscription on her grave in St. James Cemetery included the following words.

Few have passed through the Vale of Life
so much the Child of hapless fortune as the deceased;
and yet possessor of mental Endowments of no ordinary kind.
Gifted with singular talents as an Artist,
thousands have been gratified
with the able productions of her pencil!

Immortalised

In death, her name endures in the novels of Charles Dickens; *Little Dorritt, Nicholas Nickleby, Martin Chuzzlewitt* and the *Old Curiosity Shop*. Thomas Hood mentions her by name in the *Mermaid of Margate*, R. S. Surtees in *Handley Cross* and Thackeray in *A Grumble about The Christmas-Books*. Her works live on and feature regularly in Sotheby auctions. They can be seen in Windsor Castle, private collections and various galleries in Liverpool and Edinburgh.

TWO

More Heroines

There is greater scope for men to be acknowledged as heroes than there is for women. War and conflict are essentially a male stage, and traditionally men and women have only been able to compete on equal terms well away from the battlefield. This chapter includes a few of the women whose endeavours have been more than a match for many men. They include Fanny Talbot, whose gift of land started off the National Trust, Mary Ann Rogers who sacrificed her own life that others may live, Frances Barkley who circumnavigated the world and was the first white woman to set foot on Hawaii, and Margaret Bondfield, the nation's first female cabinet minister.

Fanny Talbot

Fanny Browne was born in Bridgwater in 1824, the daughter of a local merchant, John Browne, and his wife Mary. Fanny married a wealthy landowner, George Talbot, through whom she inherited considerable property on his death. One such property was at Tyn-yffynon, high in Snowdonia overlooking Barmouth on the Welsh coast, with beautiful views of the Mawddach estuary and the magnificent summit of Cader Idris.

This is a wonderful length of coastline but, despite its charms, Fanny had a particular love for four and a half acres of rough grazing enclosed in dry stone walls, set on the cliffside above Barmouth and known as the Cliff of Light or 'Dinas Oleu'. It wasn't just the countryside she loved, it was also the people. As a benefactor to the poor, founder of the local library and a supporter of many good causes, she was a well respected member of the small community where she spent her final fifty years.

Fanny was a keen artist, often sketching the local scenery. This was a skill she passed on to her son, Quartus. Fanny was also a friend of John Ruskin, the educational reformer with new ideas on art. Through this friendship, Fanny arranged for Quartus to be taught art at Oxford. He soon became a recognised water-colourist but died after catching a cold on an expedition to the Lake District. Fanny was devastated at the loss of the only heir to her estate. With typical generosity, in 1876 Fanny gifted to Ruskin a row of ten cottages, cleft in the mountainside below her own cottage, to be used for a co-operative housing scheme. However Ruskin never once visited the site nor took an interest in its affairs. Fanny had been considering donating Dinas Oleu to Ruskin but now changed her mind.

Amongst Fanny's visitors was Hardwicke Rawnsley, who with Robert Hunter and Octavia Hill, were the co-founders of the National Trust. All were friends with Fanny for they moved in the same charitable and learned circles. On one such visit, Hardwicke was reading to Fanny his proposed agenda for the first meeting of the Trust, not yet an organisation with a property to its name. Fanny seized the opportunity. She declared that the Trust was the very thing she had been looking for. She was concerned that if she passed Dinas Oleu onto an individual, it would not be kept sacrosanct. She was determined that it should not be disfigured with asphalt paths and cast iron seats, as had happened in so many open park areas. She asked Rawnsley to accept Dinas Oleu into the Trust's safe keeping.

And so on 29 March 1895, the Trust took possession of its very first property, an inspiration for others to follow, the generous gift of that Somerset lady. Fanny passed away in June 1917, aged 93, and was buried on the Welsh coast at Llanaber Church.

Mary Ann Rogers

In Liverpool's Anglican Cathedral, a stained glass window depicts various heroic women, including Mary Ann Rogers. In Southampton, opposite the Royal Pier, a drinking fountain also recognises the bravery of this lady. But in Somerset, she is almost forgotten. Mary Ann Foxwell was born in Dyehouse Close Lane in Frome in February 1855. Her parents were James, a slaughter man, and Sophia. In 1876 she married a sailor called Richard Rogers, who drowned within a few years when swept overboard in the Channel, leaving Mary with two children. To support her family, Mary became a ship's stewardess on a steamer which sailed between Southampton and the Channel Islands. It was a career which was to lead to her tragic death against a backdrop of courage and self sacrifice.

The tragedy unfolded when the London and South Western Railway Company advertised a day trip to the Channel Islands on board the *Stella*, a single funnelled steamer. It was shortly before midday on 30 March 1899 when the *Stella* set sail. Even though fair weather turned to fog within two hours of sailing, Captain Reeks maintained full speed. Eight miles off the coast of Alderney, he sighted rocks on the starboard bow and swung the ship's wheel to port. But it was too late; the racing tide dragged the ship onto the Casquet Rocks, where she sank within ten minutes of grounding.

During that time, lifebelts were distributed amongst the passengers. The women and children were boarded into the lifeboats as the first priority. Mary Ann Rogers gathered all the ladies together and quietly took command, ensuring each of them had a life jacket, even fastening them for those whose fingers were too frail or shaking with fear. Seeing that all gathered were now correctly fitted out, she began to put on her own life jacket when she realised one particular passenger was missing. The late arrival came hurrying onto deck without a lifejacket. By now, the group of ladies were descending into the lifeboats. Quickly removing her own life jacket, Mary slipped it onto her passenger and made sure she safely descended the ladder.

As she looked down, she realised the boats were full but the sailors were not pulling away. They were waiting for Mary to make the descent into a boat. Afraid that it might capsize if she boarded it, she urged the sailors to pull away before the lifeboats were sucked down with the sinking ship. Leaning over the side, she waved as she shouted goodbye. So short was the time available that only six of the lifeboats were launched, two of these as the ship was sinking.

Within minutes, the lifeboats were clear and the *Stella* sank. As the ship went down, Mary Ann Rogers was seen to raise her hands to heaven, cry 'Lord, have me' and then sink with the ship. Hers was not the only life lost that day. Of the two hundred and seventeen passengers and crew, a hundred and four others perished.

At the dedication of the window in Liverpool Cathedral in 1909, the Reverend William McNeill declared, 'Mary Ann Rogers achieved fame not by the labour of a lifetime but by one heroic deed. In the last five minutes of her life with a dying hand she grasped it, rescuing herself from oblivion, and winning for herself a place among this goodly company of the Staircase Window. It is true of her, literally true, that nothing in her life became her like the leaving of it.'

Frances Barkley

Rare indeed were sea-going women in the late eighteenth century, other than perhaps as stowaways. Shipwrecks, piracy, wars and tempest all made life at sea a precarious business, especially for those adventurers who traded in the newly discovered territories. But that was the world of Frances Barkley, the first European woman to set foot on Hawaii, British Columbia and Alaska, and one of the first women to circumnavigate the world.

Frances Hornby Trevor was born one of twins in Bridgwater in 1769 and was christened there in St. Mary's Church. Her mother, who already had two older daughters, died whilst Frances was still an infant and her twin sister, Elizabeth, died aged seven. Her father, the Reverend Doctor John Trevor, was the Rector of Otterhampton near Bridgwater and was later to marry again, this time to Miss Harriet Smith, a Bridgwater lady by whom he had four sons. He travelled extensively, taking his wife and children with him. Gradually it became apparent that whilst the rest of the family and servants suffered from sea sickness, Frances was able to sleep for hours in her berth. Perhaps this was a sign of her affinity with the sea.

When Frances was a year old, Captain Cook discovered New Zealand. He discovered Hawaii when she was nine and was killed there by the natives when she was ten. This was the age of discovery and Frances's travels had already begun. Aged seventeen, she was staying temporarily in Ostend where her father was acting as the chaplain to the English community. She was a beautiful young lady, slim built and with red-gold hair which flowed down her back. Convent educated, she had a good knowledge of the French language. Hardly surprising then that this well-spoken, well educated and pleasing young lady should attract the attention of a sea captain who, in September 1786, had just arrived aboard the newly built ship *Loudoun*. It was his first command as captain following years of trading in the Far East and the West Indies.

Captain Charles William Barkley was twenty-six-years-old when he reached Ostend and within weeks, in October 1786, he married Frances at her father's church, her father performing the service. Six weeks later they set sail on a journey which was to be the first of two that took them to the north-west coast of North America, trading for the Bengal Fur Company in the pelts of sea otters, Barkley having invested £3,000 of his own money in the venture.

The change of life style for Frances could not have been more dramatic, from convent educated vicar's daughter to the ocean-going wife of a sea captain destined for the unexplored west coast of America. Within days they were sailing into a storm during which her husband was critically ill with rheumatic fever. He recovered in time to see his ship safely around the treacherous waters of the infamous Cape Horn.

In May 1787 they made landfall at Hawaii and Frances became the first European woman to reach those shores. Natives canoed out to the ship in order to trade. The reception was friendlier than that received by Captain Cook just a few years before and Frances acquired a native girl called Winée to remain with her as a servant. With fresh food and water on board, the *Imperial Eagle,* as the ship had been renamed, sailed to the north-west coast of America.

In June they reached British Columbia. Once again, Frances was to be the first European woman to set foot on those shores. Trade for Captain Barkley was excellent. His was the first of three ships to arrive and he was able to purchase all the furs available at the lowest prices. On their arrival, they moored in Friendly Cove on Vancouver Island and were visited by a stranger in a canoe. He was exceedingly dirty and cloaked in greasy sea-otter skins. To their amazement, he boarded the ship and introduced himself as Dr. John Mackey, a former ship's surgeon, who, having lived with the Indians for the last year, had 'gone native'. As scruffy as he appeared, he was an excellent ally in effecting trade with the local Indians.

A month was spent in Friendly Cove before they sailed to the south east. As new territory was discovered and charted, Captain Barkley gave names to the most relevant places discovered. Barkley Sound he named after himself, with Frances Island and Hornby Peak after his wife. The dangers involved in exploring such undiscovered lands was brought home when the Captain anchored his ship in the calm waters between an island and the shore. A long boat was launched to explore a small river in the hope of finding Indians with whom to trade. Twelve men went with a smaller boat in tow. When the river became too shallow for the long boat, six men continued up the river in the smaller boat – never to return. The following day, a large armed contingent went ashore only to discover the torn and bloody clothing of their former crew members, killed by the Indians. What happened to their bodies remains unknown, but years later other traders in the same area were offered the shrivelled hand of a European and one Indian was seen to be wearing the seal of one of the lost crew members as an earring.

Charles Barkley headed east for Macao where the highest prices could be reached selling furs to the Chinese. Eight hundred skins were traded in return for the equivalent of 30,000 dollars. With their trading complete, the Barkleys sailed with a fresh cargo on to the island of Mauritius. Unfortunately whilst there, Captain Barkley discovered that as the result of legal action between his ship's owners and the East India Company, the *Imperial Eagle* had been confiscated. So the following year was spent in Mauritius and it was there that their first child, a son called William Hippolyte Andrew Barkley, was born.

Returning to England, they were shipwrecked off the coast of France. The family of three suddenly found themselves alone on the ship with just two servants, the entire crew having taken to the boats and disappeared. It was night and the ship's bottom had been ripped open, and only their cargo of cotton kept them afloat long enough to be towed to safety. It was just a matter of days short of two years from when they sailed from Ostend that they finally stepped ashore at Portsmouth. Frances had become the second woman to have circumnavigated the world: the first was French and had completed the voyage as a stowaway disguised as a man.

In 1791 Captain Barkley was given command of the *Princess Frederica* and the family of three set sail for India, The three became four during the voyage when a daughter, Martha, was born during a violent storm off the Cape of Good Hope. In Calcutta they transferred to the *Halcyon* and were once more bound for the north west coast of America. Weather on the voyage was atrocious and for ten days they suffered the battering of a hurricane. The conditions for the two young children were appalling. Disease struck the ship. Charles was close to death for several days and had to be restrained by the crew to stop him harming himself during his fits of delirium. Within days, their youngest child was similarly struck down and died the day before her first birthday. She was buried later on the Dutch island of Celebes.

The snow-capped Mount St Elias provided them with their first view of Alaska. Frances, now the first European woman to set foot on that territory, was able to spend much time ashore and was surprised to see considerable evidence of crop cultivation. But not all aspects of their visit were quite so civilised. One evening, the night watch aboard the *Halcyon* sighted a number of war canoes approaching. They gave the impression of being a raiding party and hence a broadside was fired across their bows. Despite such difficulties, it was a profitable trip and when they sailed for Hawaii, the ship contained a full cargo of sea otter pelts. The Barkleys found that trade was more difficult on this second voyage, the islanders having higher expectations. But they were delighted to find that a pair of turkeys they had presented to the island chief on their first visit had increased in numbers, and herein lies Frances's claim that she introduced turkeys to Hawaii. The turkeys in fact were so highly prized by the islanders that, rather than being eaten, they were used as gifts to settle accounts when serious wrongs needed to be addressed.

From Hawaii they sailed to Vietnam. As they sailed the coast of China, they were boarded and captured by the Chinese. Frances and her young son were taken ashore as prisoners and made to sit while a huge crowd of women gathered around them to stand and stare at these strange looking foreigners. Inquisitive as to Frances' hair style, they began to pull at the pins which held it in place. As the pins were pulled, her hair cascaded down to her waist like a golden waterfall. The effect on the Chinese was stunning. Such was the impact, that they believed her to be a goddess, and Frances and her son were released and allowed to continue their journey.

On reaching Vietnam, they sailed forty miles up river to Saigon. On their second day there, a splendid looking prow approached bringing a deputation from the king requesting their presence at his palace. It was a great honour to be invited and they were escorted by a large armed guard to keep the crowd at bay. It appeared that Frances was the first European women ever to visit their country.

From Vietnam they sailed on to Mauritius, unaware that it had been captured by the French who were now at war with England. The *Halcyon* was confiscated as a prize and its captain and crew taken prisoner. The Barkleys remained in Mauritius for a year and were eventually released on parole. They returned to England on board the *Betsy*. Their second global circumnavigation had taken four and a half years to complete. It was November 1794 and at last the family was to settle down. The remainder of Frances' life was spent in England, where the couple raised two more daughters and three more sons. Charles died in 1832 and Frances in May 1845.

It was the end of an era. Frances had lived through the age of discovery, through years of high adventure, crossing the world's oceans under sail, visiting lands where no European woman had previously ventured. She had faced pirates, hostile natives, storm, tempest and tropical diseases. She had twice circumnavigated the globe, surely the first woman ever to do so. And she was still only twenty five years old when she finally settled down to family life on dry land.

As a postscript to her story, in 1958 the 128 foot merchant vessel *Rennsoy* was launched from Stavanger in Norway. In 1990 she was purchased by 'Lady Rose Charter Marine Services' to carry tourists along the British Columbian coast. She was renamed, and remains, the *Frances Barkley* in honour of the lady from Somerset.

Margaret Bondfield

There was a time when the Suffragette movement had to fight for the right of women to vote, let alone enter the world of politics. There were many heroines during the movement's pioneering period, but they in turn were followed by more ladies of outstanding ability and commitment. One was Margaret Bondfield, who was not only an MP but the first woman to become a cabinet minister.

Margaret was born at Hunts Place in Chard in 1873, the daughter of William and Anne Bondfield. Anne was the daughter of a Wesleyan minister and raised her children to follow her strong radical views. William Bondfield was a textile worker, also well known for his radical views, which inevitably he passed on to Margaret, who was the tenth of their eleven children. When the firm closed for which her father had worked for forty years, the lack of money left the family facing considerable difficulties.

Margaret's schooling was short-lived. Aged thirteen, she taught in the local boys' school and the following year began working as a draper's assistant in a Brighton store. It was a close knit family business which maintained personal links with its customers. Unfortunately the workforce, who lived in, did not enjoy the same privileges in respect of their living accommodation.

Margaret shared a dormitory with many others. It was on the top floor of the house and suffered from cold in the winter and being stiflingly hot in the summer. There was little privacy, not even for washing, and strict rules existed about not entering the dormitory during the day time. Margaret was experiencing the plight of many lower paid shop assistants.

It was at this time that she met Louisa Martindale, a regular customer at the store, and the two women became friends. Louisa was a campaigner for women's rights and a ready listener to the hardships faced by working class women. Margaret found comfort in being able to tell someone else about her unhappiness, spending what little free time she had at Louisa's home with other women in a similar situation. Louisa was Margaret's first introduction to someone from a more cultured and wealthier background than her own, treating her on level terms as a friend and not as a servant. Through the relationship, Margaret was exposed to social history and the concerns which she later brought to her political career.

Aged nineteen, she moved to London. Despite the testimonials which she carried with her, describing her as 'a thoroughly smart business young person', she took three months to find employment. She became a shop assistant but once again found the working conditions unacceptable. On learning of the formation of the National Union of Shop Assistants, she became a member and was soon elected to its district council. In 1898 Margaret became the assistant secretary to the Union, a position she held for ten years, and contributed many articles to the Union journal under the pen-name Grace Dare. One which caused a minor sensation was based on her views that married couples should be equal not only in their right to work but in sharing the household chores, highly controversial in the 1890's.

By 1899 she was serving as the only woman delegate to the Trades Union Congress. It was a man's world and she later claimed that she learnt to smoke as a defence against the smell of the men's pipes. Sharing platforms with great orators like Keir Hardy and Ramsay MacDonald, this dark-haired, bright-eyed lady cut an impressive figure. Her distinctive, resonant voice, with a somewhat musical quality; her confident delivery, which reminded some of her listeners of a courageous robin, more than compensated for her small physical stature.

During those early years in the Trade Union movement, she carried out a two year study of working conditions for the Women's Industrial Council. The survey required a wide range of experience. With each change of employer, her references became deliberately shorter and the positions she filled reflected a downward path. Whilst her career as a shop assistant was in decline, her experience of politics was growing rapidly.

In 1898, she produced a paper on the pay and conditions of shop workers. She was now recognised as an authority on the subject, occasionally being called upon to serve on governmental select committees where matters of industrial relations were concerned.

In 1908 she took up the post of secretary of the Women's Labour League. At the same time, she worked within the Women's Co-operative movement fighting for a minimum wage and better conditions for children to combat the relatively high child mortality rate. Two years later her work on the Health Insurance Bill ensured the inclusion of maternity benefits.

She continued her campaign for total suffrage and her views, considered by many as extreme, often brought her into conflict. Independently minded, she opposed the bill for female emancipation, which was supported by her Labour colleagues, feeling it was too limited and fell well short of total adult suffrage. She campaigned against the recruitment of men to fight in the First World War, arguing that a negotiated settlement was preferred, an opinion viewed by many as unpatriotic.

She became increasingly active in the Labour movement and from 1918 to 1921 served on the executive. In 1923, as MP for Northampton, she was one of the first women to enter parliament. The following year she was appointed Parliamentary Secretary in the Ministry of Labour, a role to which she was ideally suited. A year later she lost her seat in the general election. In 1926 she bounced back as the MP for Wallsend, once again serving under Ramsey MacDonald. It was he who appointed her as Minister of Labour. She had become the first ever female cabinet minister and the first woman to be sworn to the Privy Council. In 1931 she lost her seat and seven years later retired from Trade Union work. Her life was then dedicated to her new roles as vice-president of the National Council of Social Service and chairman of the Women's Group on Public Welfare.

In her later years, her health began to fail but she maintained her keen interest in politics and enjoyed the pleasures of her country garden. In 1929, she was awarded an honorary doctorate from Bristol University and the following year granted the freedom of Chard. In her retirement, she was appointed Companion of Honour.

Throughout her life, during which she remained unmarried, she maintained the strong Christian belief which had always been the driving force behind her determination to improve life for others. Her autobiography, *A Life's Work* (1949), reflects her modesty in concentrating on the causes she supported rather than her considerable personal achievements. Aged 80, she died in London in June 1953.

THREE

Defending the Empire

The Crimean War 1854 – 1856

Queen Victoria instituted the Victoria Cross by Royal Warrant in 1856, but it was made retrospective to the autumn of 1854 to cover the Crimean War. The war was one in which the British and French combined forces to help the Turks against the Russians. In the early part of 1854, thousands of British troops were sent to the Crimea. Lt. Daniel Clutterbuck of Bath sailed on board the *Echunga*. Bridgwater's Denis Heron, a sergeant in the 4th Light Dragoons, sailed on the steamship *Simla* along with Lord Lucan and the 8th Hussars. With the 11th Hussars was Glastonbury born Private Edward Wilcox. It was September when they arrived, only to be struck by cholera and losing hundreds of men in the weeks that followed, before seeing action at the Battles of the Alma, Sebastopol and Balaclava.

On 24 October the day began with the usual 6 o'clock morning parade. After completing various duties, Sergeant Heron was sitting outside his tent writing home to his parents. Suddenly a small round shot hit the ground close by, embedding itself in the grass. Denis rapidly put away pen and paper as the trumpets sounded the 'mount'. The day's fighting had begun.

Charge of the Light Brigade

Up on the Causeway Heights, ten thousand Russian troops advanced onto gun positions held by just five hundred Turks. Their capture left the British cavalry dangerously exposed to shelling from the higher ground. Lord Lucan withdrew his troops to a safer position. Denis Heron requested permission to rejoin his regiment instead of completing his guard duty. Having found a volunteer from the sick list to take his place, he was allowed to join his fellow troopers. Leaping into the saddle, he rode off at a gallop to rejoin his unit. Meanwhile up on the Heights, overlooking the half mile wide North Valley, the Russians were now capturing British guns and setting up the gun positions that the Light Brigade would soon be commanded to attack. On one side the Russians held the Causeway Heights with artillery and infantry. On the opposite side were the Fedioukine Hills, also now held by the Russians with artillery and infantry. At the top end of the valley were the heavy Russian guns with the Light Brigade at the bottom end.

The realization that the Russians were towing away captured British guns galvanised the British commander-in-chief, Lord Raglan, into action. He instructed General Airey to write an order to be taken to Lord Lucan, commander of the cavalry. 'Lord Raglan wishes the cavalry to advance rapidly to the front - follow the enemy and try to prevent the enemy carrying away the guns. Troop Horse Artillery may accompany. French cavalry is on your left. Immediate. (Sgd.) Airey.'

The order was carried by the doomed Captain Nolan, a first class horseman who rapidly descended the slopes down to the Light Brigade. He was impetuous, even reckless, but achieved the task at breakneck speed. As he rode, Raglan shouted to him 'Tell Lord Lucan the cavalry is to attack immediately'.

The fateful message
Nolan reached the brigade, shouting as he went 'Boys, we'll soon have something to do' and handed the order to Lucan: 'Lord Raglan's orders are that the cavalry are to attack immediately'.

From Raglan's position on the Heights, the intention of the message was obvious. He could see the Russians, he could see them removing the British guns on the Heights. From Lucan's position, at the bottom of the valley, he could only look up the slope to where the Cossacks had placed their own guns at the head of the valley, with artillery ready to fire into it from either side. He could not see the gun positions high up on the Heights and was oblivious to the actual meaning of Raglan's message.

The order made no sense. How was artillery to be attacked by cavalry, and with no infantry in support?

'Attack, sir?' questioned Lucan having carefully read the order, 'Attack what? What guns, sir?'.

The impatient and impetuous Nolan threw back his head and waved an arm in the air in a vague suggestion of a general direction.

'There, my lord, is your enemy. There are your guns.' And thus Nolan, who now rode over to join the 17th Lancers, doomed the Light Brigade to their fate.

Lucan passed the instruction on to Cardigan, commander of the Light Brigade, and ordered him to advance on the Russian guns whilst he brought up the rear with the Heavy Brigade. Cardigan reluctantly accepted the command. Sergeant Heron and his fellow troopers were finishing off their rations and quenching their thirsts when the order to mount was given. Their officer, Lord George Paget, had just lit a cigar. 'You will take command of the second line,' Cardigan informed Paget, 'and I expect your best support - mind, your best support'.

Into the valley

Cardigan galloped to the front and ordered two lines to form up. In the first were the 13th Light Dragoons, 17th Lancers and the 11th Hussars with Glastonbury's Private Edward Wilcox. This was the line which would be the first to be exposed to the devastating volleys from the Russian guns. The 4th Light Dragoons, with Bridgwater's Denis Heron, and the 8th Hussars with Bath's Lt. Daniel Clutterbuck made up the second line of attack.

Cardigan, now some yards out in front, drew his sword and the trumpet sounded. 'The brigade will advance,' he bellowed. The Light Brigade moved off, shortly followed by the slower Heavy Brigade, into a three sided trap. To their left were eight battalions of Russian cavalry and fourteen guns; to the right were eleven battalions and thirty guns and facing them the Russian cavalry in three lines with twelve guns and six squadrons of lancers. Six hundred and seventy-three members of the Light Brigade entered the valley; confident, bold, courageous and eager to do battle.

The first casualties

Within minutes of the advance the Russian guns opened fire. Smoke and dust rose at the lower end of the valley. Slowly it dawned on the onlookers that the Light Brigade was on its way to its destruction.

Rapidly the pace quickened as round shot and shells flew into the ranks from three sides, creating huge gaps as the dead and wounded fell. 'Close in. Close in,' commanded the individual officers. Obediently the Light Brigade closed the ranks and continued their advance into the valley, increasing their speed to a gallop and yelling as they went.

Carnage

All the brigade could see at the end of the valley was a wall of white smoke and flame-red flashes as the guns let loose their deadly assault. As each victim fell, the troopers either side would swerve to avoid their fallen colleague only to close the gap immediately after. Up on the Heights, an old soldier broke into tears as he watched the carnage. The French General Bosquet, struck by the bravery and futility, simply said, in words that have lost none of their poignancy, 'C'est magnifique mais ce n'est pas la guerre'.

As the first line approached the Russian guns, another volley let loose. Scores fell, the first line disappeared in its entirety. Glastonbury's Edward Wilcox was amongst the wounded and began the struggle back to the British lines. Lord Lucan, bringing up the Heavy Brigade at the rear, declared he was not going to risk his men against such odds and withdrew out of range of the Russian guns.

At the front, the air was filled with the terrifying screams of injured horses and men. As Heron advanced, his horse leaping over fallen men and horses, he witnessed the carnage but remained focused on his objective, to capture the Russian guns. Ahead of him were the 13th Light Dragoons with Lieutenant Percy Smith at the fore. Smith was a charismatic character who had previously lost one arm but still cheered his men on and took only a small wound as he charged through the Russian guns with his dragoons right behind him. Of all the horses in the 13th, his was one of only two which escaped unharmed.

Denis Heron enters the fray

A period of carnage followed as men and horses fell victim to shot, shell and sabre. Only fifty men survived from the first line. It was all happening so quickly. Denis Heron and Lt. Clutterbuck were soon facing the Russian cannons, which appeared only at the last moment through the haze of smoke. Charging into the fiery inferno, batteries of massed rifles scythed out gaps in their ranks. Clutterbuck was slightly wounded when a shell fragment hit his right foot but was able to continue until his horse was shot from beneath him. In fact only two of the horses from the 8th Hussars were to return unscathed.

Once past the guns, the hand to hand fighting began. The pall of smoke surrounding them obscured all sunlight. For Heron, it was impossible to tell how the battle was going other than in his own immediate area. But all around him his comrades were falling, killed or seriously wounded.

Success for Denis Heron

The 4th Light Dragoons fought like tigers. Captain Alexander Low, fighting as though possessed, killed thirteen Russian gunners on his own. And Denis Heron was not without his own success. Attacked by a Russian lancer, he wheeled his horse around as the lancer's thrust landed low, passing through the sheepskin beneath his saddle. The lancer tried again. Once more Denis wheeled, striking out with his sabre and mortally wounding his attacker. Another Russian took his place, one of stronger stock and a good swordsman. Denis however was a master of the sabre and forced his attacker from the saddle. He then cut down the gunners on a Russian artillery piece and along with two other troopers captured both the gun and its six horses. Unfortunately, the Cossack trained horses would not respond to instructions in English and the gun had to be abandoned.

All in all, the 4th Light Dragoons secured and silenced the guns and then continued to press forward. In so doing they met the retreating 11th Hussars. There were no more than seventy men between the two groups and the mass of the Russian cavalry was now charging down on them.

Lord George Paget rallied his men together. 'Halt front. If you don't front, my boys, we are done,' he shouted. They halted and formed up, just as they had so many times in parade drills, ready to attack the Russian mass. Then they became aware of another advancing force just five hundred yards to their rear and cutting off their only means of retreat. They looked for Cardigan for instructions. He was long gone. 'No part of a general's duty to fight the enemy among private soldiers,' he later explained.

The long walk back

Heedless of the odds, Lord Paget commanded and his seventy men obeyed. They charged the Russian cavalry who were cutting off their retreat. What could have been going through Denis Heron's mind as he surely rode to his death? But as they attacked the Russians with what little energy and strength they had left, the Russians halted and gave way, limply jabbed their lances at the survivors. And so, either through Russian compassion or perhaps exhaustion, the surviving few pushed through the enemy cavalry and began the journey back between the artillery and infantry that still lined the valley on either side.

At the other end of the valley, Cardigan surveyed the scene. Looking across the valley floor, littered with dead and dying, came the remains of the Light Brigade. They straggled along in ones and twos, mostly walking wounded, only a few still mounted, some being led back draped over saddles. Almost every horse able to carry a load had been given up to carry the wounded. 'What a scene of havoc was this last mile, strewn with the dead and dying and all friends!' Lord Paget wrote later. Sergeant Heron knew that his day would not be over until they reached the safety of their own lines. Even now the Russian guns still fired, relentless in their brutality.

As they limped back, Sergeant Heron was hit by a bullet which passed through his left arm. Weakened even further through loss of blood, he finally made it back to his own lines. For Denis Heron, the battle was over. For Raglan, Cardigan and Lucan, the battle of words had just begun. Of the six hundred and seventy-three who entered the fray, only one hundred and ninety three returned to their lines. The majority of these returned on foot. Five hundred horses had been killed in the action. Each returning group was welcomed with cheers and warm embraces from those who had already reached the lines. The whole episode had lasted a mere twenty minutes from trumpet call to the return of the last survivor.

That same evening, with numerous other wounded, Heron was transferred to a steamer bound for a hospital in Constantinople. For the entire five day voyage he lay in an exposed position on the deck, albeit one that was probably healthier than in the overcrowded berths below. In November, Florence Nightingale and thirty-eight nurses arrived, and Heron was nursed by the legendary lady herself during the six months he spent in Constantinople. Having been invalided to Malta he was subsequently sent home. Back in England he was taken to Netley Hospital. There, as he was always proud to relate, he was

A miniature self portrait of Sarah Biffen
(1784-1850), probably painted in the early
1820s when her reputation was at its
height and she had her own London
studio on the Strand. This is work
of the highest standard, and of
remarkable quality for someone
born without arms or legs.

The drawing below by Pat
Frost shows Sarah Biffen at work.
She held her paint brush in her
mouth and passed the handle end
through a loop on her shoulder.

1

Mary Ann Rogers (1855-1899), the Frome-born ship's stewardess who gave up her lifebelt and lost her life when the Channel Island steamer *Stella* struck the rocks off Alderney with the loss of 105 lives.

There is a memorial to her in a stained glass window in Liverpool's Anglican Cathedral, and a drinking fountain in Southampton. In Somerset she is all but forgotten.

An artist's impression from *The Illustrated London News* of the scene on board the *Stella* after she struck The Casquets off Alderney. Mary Ann Rogers is on the right.

Margaret Bondfield (1873-1953), who was born in Chard, the daughter of a textile worker and one of eleven children. She began her working life in a drapery store and ended it as Britain's first woman cabinet minister and a Companion of Honour.

ABOVE 'The Charge of the Light Brigade', a detail from the painting by Richard Caton Woodville.

LEFT Sergeant Denis Heron (1829-1895) of the 4th Light Dragoons was one of the 193 survivors of the doomed Charge. After being nursed by Florence Nightingale, he returned from the Crimea to Bridgwater.

Denis Heron's grave in Bridgwater's Bristol Road Cemetery. It was my discovery of his grave, then dilapidated and un-cared for, that inspired me to begin the research that finally led to this book. His grave was restored with funding from the Queens Royal Hussars and rededicated in 1998. A lone piper from Denis Heron's old regiment played a lament.

LEFT Major Frederick Elton (1832-1888) of Whitestaunton, near Chard, who won the Victoria Cross driving back the Russians from trenches at Sebastopol during the Crimean War.

OPPOSITE TOP
A dramatic but undoubtedly romanticised engraving of Lieutenant (later Major General) George Renny (1825-1887) of the Bengal Horse Artillery winning his Victoria Cross during the Indian Mutiny in 1857.

OPPOSITE BELOW
A cigarette card of about 1900 showing John Crimmin (1859-1945), a surgeon in the Indian Army, fighting off bandits in Burma in 1889, an action which won him the Victoria Cross. Crimmin is now buried in Wells Cemetery.

The defence of the mission station at Rorke's Drift in South Africa is the most celebrated episode in the Zulu Wars, and was immortalized in the film *Zulu*, starring Michael Caine and Stanley Baker.

The defence of the mission was led by Lt. John Rouse Merriott Chard (1847-1897) of the 24th Regiment, who was one of the 11 men later awarded the Victoria Cross.

Chard lies buried in Hatch Beauchamp churchyard, close to the porch.

honoured with a visit by Queen Victoria who was pleased to shake his hand.

In September 1855, Sebastopol was taken after heavy bombardment. The allies had taken the city but had lost 250,000 men in the course of the war. Somerset men had proved their valour and worth throughout this campaign.

About the Somerset men in the Charge of the Light Brigade

Lt Daniel Clutterbuck was born in Bath in 1823, the second son of Thomas Clutterbuck who had himself served with the Royal Horse Guards. He was promoted to Captain in the wake of the Charge and retired in 1855 when he married Sophia Ellen Spicer. They had five sons and three daughters.

Private Wilcox was born in Glastonbury and prior to enlistment in 1835 with the 11th Hussars he worked as a servant. He was wounded in the Charge but continued in active service until April 1855. He spent that and the next month in hospital and died at camp in Kadikoi in June.

Sergeant Denis Heron was born in 1829 in County Kildare, Ireland, and at the time of the battle his parents lived in Athlone, County Westmeath. Although Irish by birth, he had adopted Bridgwater as his home and spent the greater part of his life there. He was eighteen years old when he enlisted. Having served with honour, he retired from the Light Brigade and took up a post with the West Somerset Yeomanry Cavalry, first as a Sergeant-Major and then latterly as a Sergeant-Instructor.

In 1857 a requisition was sent from Bridgwater to Lord Panmure, as a result of which the town was presented with a Russian cannon captured in the Crimean War. It was placed right outside Denis Heron's front door in Salmon Parade.

After his retirement, he became the agent for the Bridgwater firm of Sutton and Co., a position he held until his death at the age of 65. He left a widow and a daughter and was buried in the Bristol Road Cemetery in Bridgwater.

It was the discovery of his dilapidated grave in 1998 that triggered my research into his story and inspired my determination to write this book. I am indebted to the Queen's Royal Hussars who responded so positively to my request for regimental funding to restore his grave and to Rob Gardner who carried out the repairs as a labour of love. The grave was re-dedicated in July 1998 by the Reverend David Arnot. A lone piper from Denis Heron's old regiment played the lament 'Flowers of the Forest'. It was a most moving moment.

Major Frederick Cockayne Elton, VC

Despite the tragic losses, the Crimean War continued. In March 1855, Somerset's twenty two year old Brevet Major Frederick Cockayne Elton, an officer in the 55th Regiment, was recognised for his courage. Major Elton had been in charge of a party of men preparing new trenches in advanced positions at Sebastopol. This was particularly dangerous work, and both the major and his men were exposed to heavy enemy fire. A group of Russians had moved into one of the newly built forward trenches and it was critical that this position should not be lost to the enemy. Major Elton volunteered to go forward. With a party of men much smaller than that of the enemy force, he drove the Russians back, taking one prisoner himself. This action earned him the Victoria Cross.

He led a similar attack later in the year when in command of a working party in the advanced trenches. He encouraged his men to work under heavy fire, even wielding a pick and shovel himself to set the best possible example. One of his men was later to comment that, 'There was not another officer in the British Army who would have done what Major Elton did that night'.

Frederick Elton was born in Whitestaunton near Chard in 1832 and joined the 55th Regiment when still only sixteen. He rose to the rank of Lieutenant Colonel and died in London in 1888 aged fifty six. He was buried in St. Andrew's churchyard at Whitestaunton where there is a memorial to his memory. His Victoria Cross is held in the Border Regiment Museum in Carlisle.

Private George Strong, VC

Elsewhere in the Sebastopol trenches, a humble, Somerset-born private, nineteen year old George Strong of the Coldstream Guards, was battling against the Russian attack when a shell landed directly in a trench close by and failed to explode. Well aware of the immediate danger to himself and his fellow soldiers, he jumped towards the shell, gathered it in his arms and threw it over the parapet. In so doing he saved the lives of all around. This clear thinking act of selfless bravery earned him the Victoria Cross.

George Strong was born in Odcombe near Yeovil in April 1833 and in 1854 travelled down to Plymouth to enlist in the Coldstream Guards. He died at Sherston Magna, near Malmesbury in Wiltshire, where he was buried in the grounds of the Church of the Holy Cross. His Victoria Cross is held at the Regimental Headquarters of the Coldstream Guards and was presented to him by Queen Victoria in the first VC investiture in Hyde Park in June 1857.

The Great Indian Mutiny

During the reign of Queen Victoria, law and order in India, the jewel in her imperial crown, was maintained by regiments largely made up of native troops commanded by British officers. These sepoys were mainly Hindu, supplemented by Sikhs and Muslims. The new Enfield rifle with which they had been issued used greased cartridges which had to be bitten to release their powder. The grease was partly animal fat; from pigs abominable to Muslims, and cows sacred to Hindus. Despite a hurried change to the cartridge, it was too late to calm the situation. At the garrison town of Meerut eighty five Indian troopers were court martialled for refusing to obey orders, stripped of their uniforms, paraded before the garrison, given long prison sentences and clapped in irons. It was a humiliation which fanned the smouldering fires of hatred across India.

In May 1857, Indian troops rose up in a bloody and vicious rebellion which became the Great Indian Mutiny. It was a cry for freedom from their British masters and one to which many Indians rallied whilst other troops, the Sikhs and Ghurkhas in particular, remained loyal. No fewer than four men with Somerset connections were to be awarded the Victoria Cross for valour during that period. Even more amazing is that all four are buried in Bath, three of them, although they died many years apart, in one cemetery.

The mutiny rapidly spread and undermanned Delhi soon came under attack. Within days, the city had fallen. In the wake of the loss of Delhi, British families were hunted down and murdered. The mutiny had to be put down and the credulity of the British Empire re-established.

British forces besieged the mutineers in Delhi. Brigadier General John Nicholson ordered the bombardment of the city. After three days, he led his troops through a breach in the Kashmir Gate bastion. Reaching the walls, scaling ladders were thrown into place. The British troops ascended with swords waving whilst the sepoys on top waited with bullet and bayonet to repel their advance. Three times the ladder parties were beaten back. Eventually those who reached the top confronted yet more rifles and bayonets. There was fierce and bloody hand to hand combat, with the British troops under clear instructions not to stop to help their fallen wounded but to keep the momentum going, and not to take any prisoners.

Herbert Taylor Reade, VC, CB
Elsewhere the Kashmir Gate had been blown apart by a team of Royal Engineers. Although few of them survived they had provided the opening through which the 52nd Foot stormed into the city along with the 61st Regiment. With the 61st was their Canadian born twenty-eight-year old surgeon, Herbert Taylor Reade, who now lies at rest in the Locksbrook Cemetery in Bath. Trapped at the end of a street, all around him lay wounded and dying soldiers which he tended to the best of his ability. But from the rooftops, where an advancing party of rebels had established themselves, shots were being fired down on the wounded as well as those still fighting. Reade drew his sword and called on the few able-bodied soldiers available to attack the rebel's rooftop position. The attack was completely successful thanks to his strong leadership. For his outstanding courage in this action he was awarded the Victoria Cross.

Within hours the British presence within the city was re-established, although fighting went on for some days until the remaining rebel troops withdrew. During that period Surgeon Reade was back in action and was one of the first through the breach in the magazine where, with the aid of a sergeant, he spiked one of the enemy's guns.

Lt. George Alexander Renny, VC
On the same day, thirty two year old Lt. George Alexander Renny of the Bengal Horse Artillery was also gaining honours. After the capture of the magazine by the British, the enemy set fire to the thatched roof of the magazine and kept up a heavy cross fire, pinning down the

British troops within. The fire was extinguished and then, despite the obvious risk to himself, George Renny went up on to the top of the magazine wall from where he flung sticks of shells with lighted fuses into the enemy. The effect was devastating and the mutineers were forced to withdraw. For valour under heavy cross fire, he was awarded the Victoria Cross.

Renny later rose to the rank of Major General and died in 1887 in Bath where he also rests in the Locksbrook Cemetery. His Victoria Cross is held at the Royal Artillery Museum at Woolwich.

Captain Henry Edward Jerome, VC

Across northern India the mutiny continued. On 3 April 1858 a lieutenant in Jerome's regiment lay severely wounded in an exposed position beneath the walls of the fort at Jhansi. Captain Henry Edward Jerome went out under heavy fire and carried the wounded lieutenant to safety. For this, and further acts of gallantry at the capture of the Fort at Chandairee, the storming of Jhansi and in action against superior rebel forces at Jumna on 28 May, where he was severely wounded, he was awarded the Victoria Cross.

Jerome retired as a Major-General and died at Bath in 1901, where his grave can be found in the Lansdown Cemetery.

Colonel William Francis Frederick Waller, VC

Yet another man with Somerset links gained glory during the mutiny, eighteen-year-old Lieutenant William Francis Frederick Waller of the 25th Bombay Infantry. Waller had been present at two earlier sieges and was now one of two European officers commanding a small force besieging the fortress town of Gwalior, which had been overrun by about 11,000 sepoys.

One day Waller's English companion officer, a Lieutenant Rose, heard laughter from behind one of the gates and realised that it offered a chance for a surprise attack whilst the guard inside were distracted. Rose and Waller approached the gate with the regimental blacksmith, who used his tremendous strength to force it open. Amazingly no one heard them enter. Another gate was opened, again undetected, then another. As he opened the sixth gate, they were discovered and yet he still managed a seventh. On reaching an archway, they were fired on by a field gun. Surviving that assault, Waller and Rose met the rebels face to face in hand to hand fighting, but the gates having been breached, the rest of their group were soon pouring into the fort. The price of victory was high. Rose was hacked to death but William Waller was awarded the Victoria Cross for his gallantry. He later rose to the rank of Colonel and died in Bath aged 45 in 1885. He is the third member of that honoured band to be buried in the Locksbrook Cemetery in Bath.

Lieutenant George Vincent Fosbery, VC

Although the Indian Mutiny had been crushed, decades of unrest were to follow on the Indian sub-continent, producing yet more Somerset holders of the Victoria Cross.

In St. Mary's Cemetery in Bath lies the grave of George Fosbery who died in 1907. He is remembered for two achievements: the heroism which earned him the Victoria Cross and the revolver which bears his name.

George Fosbery was a lieutenant in the 4th Bengal European Regiment when in October 1863 he was with a party which had been sent to relieve a fort in North West India. Enemy forces had captured the area surrounding the fort, killing sixty of the British forces and driving the remainder back inside. Just two narrow paths led up to the top of the crag on which the fort was sited. Occasional rocks provided cover for no more than one or two men at a time.

Lieutenant Colonel Keyes was in command of the small force attempting to retake the crag. He took part of the force up one path leaving George Fosbery to lead an attack up the other. Despite his men coming under fire, Fosbery did this with great coolness and was the first to reach the top of the crag. Keyes himself was wounded, leaving Fosbery in overall command. Gathering the two groups together, Fosbery renewed the attack on the enemy until they were completely routed, earning himself the Victoria Cross.

After retiring as a Lieutenant-Colonel in 1876, George Fosbery devoted himself to perfecting the machine gun. Amongst his other developments was an automatic revolver which was marketed as the Webley-Fosbery .455. A Webley-Fosbery Colt .38 was also produced and he even developed an exploding bullet intended to help infantry and artillery to determine their range.

In 1997 his Victoria Cross came under the auctioneer's hammer at a sale in Canada, and was purchased by an unknown bidder for the sum of $45,000.

John Crimmin, VC

During the mid 1880's, the British were expanding their territories in Burma. The years from 1887 to 1889 were then spent suppressing resistance which came from well organised and often large bandit armies.

Twenty-nine-year-old Dublin born John Crimmin was serving as a member of the Bombay Medical Service with the Indian Army. It was New Year's Day 1889 when a British lieutenant and four soldiers ran into a large group of bandits near Lwekaw in Eastern Karenni. Two of the British group lay wounded. John Crimmin, as a surgeon, rushed to their assistance. Concealed in a cluster of trees, the bandit forces put Crimmin under heavy fire. Ignoring the shots all around him, he saw to the needs of one of the wounded until the enemy fire became so intense he was obliged to join in the action to protect his patients.

When the fire subsided, he attended to his second patient. Just then the enemy attacked in considerable force and rushed John Crimmin as he tended the wounded soldiers. He thrust his sword into one man and then set about a second whilst a sepoy, fighting at his side, shot a third. With the remainder in flight, John Crimmin returned to his patients. For his courage under fire, he was awarded the Victoria Cross. His action as he ran his sword through one of the bandit force was illustrated in a series of cigarette cards published around 1900 depicting British heroes.

He retired as a Colonel and died in February 1945. What brought him to Somerset is unknown but he now lies buried in Wells Cemetery.

Samuel Vickery, VC

Samuel Vickery was born in 1873 at Combe St Nicholas near Chard and enlisted into the army at the age of twenty. In 1897 he was sent to India to join the Dorset Regiment, then fighting tribesmen in the hostile North West corner of India. During the course of a skirmish, one of his comrades was shot and lay wounded at the bottom of a slope. With little regard for his own safety, Samuel Vickery ran down the slope, continuously under heavy fire, picked up the injured soldier, carrying him to safety. For this he was awarded the Victoria Cross.

Following a later episode in which he was wounded, he returned to England where, whilst recovering at Netley Abbey, Queen Victoria presented him with his Victoria Cross. But that was not the end of Samuel Vickery's military adventures. During the Boer War he was captured by the Boers and made a successful and daring escape. And he was in the thick of the fighting again at the Battle of Ypres in the First World War. He finally settled in Cardiff where he passed away in June 1952.

The Zulu Wars and Rorke's Drift

Lieutenant John Rouse Merriott Chard, VC

South east of Taunton lies the small village of Hatch Beauchamp. In its church is a window which honours Lieutenant John Rouse Merriott Chard, VC, hero of Rorke's Drift during the Zulu Wars, an episode immortalised in the classic film *Zulu*, starring Michael Caine and Stanley Baker. The window is best viewed from within the church and for those prepared to make the pilgrimage, his grave can easily be found on the south side of the church.

John Chard was born in 1847. Aged twenty-one, he was commissioned into the Royal Engineers. A spell in Bermuda and then Malta preceded his transfer to South Africa, early in 1879, where the Governor of the Cape Colony, Sir Bartle Frere, was planning a British invasion of Zululand, then still an independent thorn in the side of British attempts to absorb South Africa into the Empire.

Sir Bartle Frere sent an ultimatum to Cetawayo, the King of the Zulu nation, demanding the disbandment of his armies by a prescribed date. The Zulus were a proud nation whose culture revolved around a military ethic. Their warriors were organised into regiments called impi, and were well trained and disciplined. Frere's deadline passed and in January 1879 the British invaded Zululand. The indecisive Lord Chelmsford was in command of 5,000 British troops supported by 8,000 Natal Kaffirs. Amongst the battalions from which his force was drawn were the Somerset Light Infantry and the South Wales Borderers.

Forces divided

Chelmsford's first mistake was to split his force in five, thus creating smaller vulnerable units from one potentially overwhelming force. He had been warned of the power of the Zulu impis but viewed them as unruly bands of natives and, albeit numbering 29,000 warriors, no fit match with their assegai spears for British military might with rifles and Gatling guns. Experienced Zulu fighters knew differently.

Two of Chelmsford's units were held back in reserve whilst the other three entered Zululand at various points along the border. Chelmsford himself remained with the central group, crossed the Buffalo River at Rorke's Drift and continued to Isandhlwana where his column pitched camp. Still ignoring advice, he thought it unnecessary to form any kind of defensive barrier around camp. Instead he again divided his forces, dispatching half to support a scouting patrol.

With the number of British in the camp reduced by half, 20,000 Zulus appeared over the horizon, perfectly formed in a wide-sweeping semi-circle. They were formed up as a main central body supported by long flanks to left and right. For the defenders, it was like facing an advancing bull square on with its head lowered and two forward pointing horns, the horns being a mile or so across. The barefoot Zulu army moved forward in perfect formation, bearing their assegai spears and shields before them. First advancing at a half run, their speed increased and in minutes the camp was completely enclosed and the impi warriors were breaking through the inadequate defences. Every officer and all but two men of the South Wales Borderer's were killed in the action. On Chelmsford's return he stated, 'I can't understand it. I left a thousand men here'. In all 858 British soldiers were killed, together with 470 of the native levies.

Rorke's Drift

The battle of Isandhlwana over, a Zulu impi of 4,500 warriors advanced the few miles to Rorke's Drift, a mission station with a chapel and the missionary's house, then held by a company of the 24th Regiment under two subalterns, Lieutenants John Chard and Gonville Bromhead. In itself, the mission was insignificant but its position close to the Buffalo River made it of strategic importance on the military supply line and it had been commandeered as a storage depot and field hospital. As the Zulus approached Rorke's Drift, they had the added benefit of the rifles and ammunition captured in the field at Isandhlwana.

At Rorke's Drift, the distant sound of rifle and cannon fire could be heard. The hospital surgeon and the Swedish priest Otto Witt, who lived at the mission with his wife and young daughter, climbed the hill at its rear to investigate. Down at the Buffalo River, Lieutenant Chard and a section of men were repairing pontoons when two breathless horsemen arrived to report the massacre at Isandhlwana. Chard sent orders back to the mission for Lieutenant Bromhead to prepare for a possible attack and then dispatched another rider to warn the garrison at Helpmekaar, some twelve miles distant.

Back at the mission, all spare ammunition was taken into the hospital and store room. These would be the points at which Chard's men would fight to the death if called upon to do so. Chard and Bromhead organized the construction of a barricade in front of the store made up from 200 lb maize bags, cases of tinned meat, teak crates and any furniture they could move in the time available. Two overturned wagons completed the defensive wall which had been created between the church and the store. Holes were knocked through walls with pick axes to permit rifle fire. The twelve patients out of the thirty five in the hospital who were well enough to hold a rifle were armed and put at the ready.

Zulu arrival

It was half past four in the afternoon when the Zulu impi appeared over the horizon and commenced their rapid but silent advance on the mission. 'Here they come, black as hell and thick as grass,' declared one soldier.

Though few in numbers, and outnumbered by thirty four to one, the defenders used the barricades they had prepared to great effect and successfully repelled the first attack. Lieutenant Chard had built the barricades deep enough to ensure that the stabbing assegai spears used by the Zulus could not effectively reach across them. This gave the British soldiers with their Martini rifles time to shoot or bayonet any Zulus attempting to breach the defences. The danger lay in the sheer numbers of attacking warriors. But as their dead fell across the barricade, so their bodies added to the distance to be crossed and the Zulus temporarily fell back.

The retreating Zulus took what shelter they could behind trees, rocks and termite nests and sniped away at those in the mission with their newly acquired rifles, causing only limited damage due to their lack of experience. Then came attack after attack over a period of twelve hours of continuous fighting. After unsuccessful attempts to storm the southern defences, the Zulus moved around to the hospital and it was here that they eventually breached the defences, breaking in through a door and killing several patients.

Bayonet and assegai
Fortunately the inner walls of the hospital were made of mud and those defending its patients took turns either to fight off the advancing Zulu warriors or to break through the mud walls with a pick axe, allowing them to move from one room to another. Their ammunition already expended, fighting was hand to hand with bayonet against assegai. Room by room they retreated, some holding back the Zulus as others knocked holes through the walls and gathered the patients, finally escaping through a window when the Zulus set fire to the building.

Meanwhile the battle was still raging outside. Chard ordered his men to retreat to the inner defences where more ammunition was available. As darkness fell, the burning mission lit the night sky. The fighting continued; rifles became too hot to touch. The sick and injured, propped up against walls or the barricades, reloaded rifles as rapidly as possible. The surgeon worked on in the open, where the wounded fell, the battle raging all around him.

As midnight approached, the besieged survivors were all suffering from intense thirst. The water cart had to be brought into the inner and final line of defence and it was essential to turn the tide, despite the overwhelming odds, if there was to be any hope of survival. And so Lieutenant Chard led a ferocious but successful attack against the Zulus who had now breached the outer defences.

Shoulder to shoulder, back to back
A further two to three hours of fighting followed with Chard's men standing shoulder to shoulder at the barricade, or back to back each time the barricade was breached. In time the momentum of the Zulu attack began to wane. By dawn the Zulu's withdrawal was all but

complete and Lieutenant Chard sent men out to finish off any Zulu wounded and to round up their weapons. Hundreds of Zulu bodies lay piled at the base of the barricades. Amazingly, within the mission only fifteen lives had been lost and twelve wounded.

The defence of Rorke's Drift thus far had been bloody but successful. But the survivors knew that the Zulus would regroup, strengthened by another impi, and there would be little chance of defending the mission again. Shortly after eight in the morning, the remnants of Chelmsford's column arrived. Rorke's Drift had been saved through an heroic defence which captured the minds and imagination of a nation who otherwise would have been reeling at the defeat suffered at Isandhlwana.

Some weeks later, Cetawayo and his warriors were brutally defeated in a decisive battle at Ulundi.

Lt. Chard recognised

The thirty one year old Lieutenant Chard had courageously led one of the most heroic stands in British military history, an event which resulted in the presentation of eleven Victoria Crosses, the largest number ever given for a single action. Chard and Bromhead justifiably became national heroes. In July 1879 Chard received his VC from Sir Garnet Wolseley at St Paul's in Zululand. Later that year he visited Queen Victoria at Balmoral.

From 1892 to 1896 John Chard served as a Lieutenant Colonel in Singapore before taking up a post in Perth in Scotland. Sadly it was there that he was found to be suffering from cancer of the tongue. In November 1897 he died at Hatch Beauchamp, where his brother was rector, and was laid to rest just outside the church wall.

Other Somerset Men at Rorke's Drift

Three other Somerset men survived the battle at Rorke's Drift. Bristol born Private George Edward Orchard worked as a shoemaker's apprentice and builder before joining the army aged eighteen. He served in both India and South Africa before his discharge in 1888. Born on 1855, he died in 1940 and was buried with military honours in Paulton cemetery.

Corporal Alfred Saxty was born at Buckland Dinham near Frome in 1860. He was quite a colourful character. Aged sixteen, he joined the army but told them he was nineteen. Several times during his eighteen year career, he rose from private to corporal, then to sergeant, only to reduced back down again for such charges as 'drunk in picquet'. He was discharged at his own request in 1895 with a 'good character' reference. He died in 1936 and is buried at St. Woolos, Newport.

Private Thomas Daw, born 1856 at Merriott, near Crewkerne, began life as a labourer before joining the army in 1877. He married Emily Westcott in Wellington 1887, the town where they raised their family. He died in 1924 and lies in an unmarked grave in Wellington cemetery.

Crete

William Job Maillard, VC

The island of Crete was occupied by Turkey as part of the Ottoman Empire from 1669 to 1898. In 1866 the Cretans revolted in an attempt to gain autonomy. The revolt was crushed but for twenty years the fighting continued. Finally, the British, French, Russians and Italians combined forces to bring stability to the island. The result was the withdrawal of Turkish troops and the annexation of Crete to Greece. But before agreement could be reached, there was period of conflict in which a Somerset man was to be recognised for his bravery.

William Job Maillard was born at Banwell in the north of Somerset in 1863. He was to become the first and only naval medical officer to be awarded the Victoria Cross. It was 6 September 1898 and at Candia, now known as Heraklion, fighting continued around the town. The British Consul and a number of others had been killed. The Telegraph Station, hospital, the British camp and the cathedral were all under attack. In the harbour, a small group of British troops was besieged in the Customs House Garrison by Turkish fighters and many of the men inside were in desperate need of medical attention.

Two parties of men from *HMS Hazard* attempted to go to their rescue, including William Maillard as surgeon. Reaching the shore, they ran for cover as bullets flew around them. Glancing back, Maillard saw that the seaman left with the boat had been shot and was in urgent need of attention; the boat was drifting away. Returning through a hail of bullets, he boarded the boat and attempted to lift the injured man in order to get him to safe cover. The man's dead weight proved too much to handle; the pitching of the boat made it impossible to lift him. Maillard was forced to leave the dying seaman and return to the rest of his party, running through a continuous hail of rifle fire. He knew there had been a few near misses but it was only when he reached a position of safety that he realised just how lucky he had been. Although amazingly uninjured himself, his clothes were riddled with bullet holes. The action earned him the Victoria Cross which in 1998 was bought at auction by a private collector for £50,000.

William Maillard died in September 1903.

The Boer War

Sir Neville Reginald Howse, VC

Neville Reginald Howse was born in 1863 in Stogursey, later training as a doctor. In 1889 he emigrated to Australia only to find himself eleven years later in South Africa serving as a lieutenant in the Army Medical Corps during the Boer War.

In 1900, near Vredefort in the Orange Free State, his unit was pursuing a party of Boers when in the skirmish that followed a young British bugler fell wounded. Howse didn't hesitate and heedless of the bullets flying around him rode out to the wounded man. His horse was killed almost immediately and he was left with no option but to carry the wounded bugler back to safety dodging bullets all the way. His action earned him the Victoria Cross.

His military career continued into the First World War where one officer described how shells and bullets were treated by him with complete disregard. To the wounded soldier he was gentleness personified. After political service in Australia, he died in London in 1930.

Henry James Knight, VC

Henry James Knight was born in Yeovil in 1878. In August 1900 he was in the 1st Battalion of the King's Regiment on active service near Van Wyk's Vlei in South Africa. He was serving as a corporal and with four other men was covering the flank of a company which was coming under heavy attack from the Boers. An orderly withdrawal was required and Knight provided covering fire as one by one his company retreated to safer positions. He kept this up for an hour, during which time two of his companions were killed and two wounded.

When it came to his turn to withdraw, he managed to get one of the wounded to safety. Meanwhile, the Boers were still advancing. All Knight could do was to abandon the wounded soldier or bodily carry him to safety. But his unit was retreating and the Boers were advancing just as rapidly. Although Knight managed to get himself and the wounded soldier back to safety, he had to carry him for a full two miles. For this action he was awarded the Victoria Cross. He later rose to the rank of captain and died in 1955.

Harry George Crandon, VC

Born in Wells in 1874, Harry Crandon was serving as a private in South Africa when, in July 1901, he rode to help another private who was not only wounded but whose horse had been shot beneath him. Both men were under heavy fire and the only solution that Crandon could think of was to give up his horse to the wounded soldier and make his own way back on foot. He helped the wounded man up into the saddle and with a slap on his rump packed him off to find safety. As fast as his legs would carry him, Crandon ran back towards his own lines for three quarters of a mile, dodging bullets and under continuous heavy fire. For this courageous act in risking his own life to save a wounded comrade he was later awarded the Victoria Cross.

FOUR

World Wars

Thought at the time to be the war to end all wars, the First World War was fought mainly in the trenches of the Western Front in Europe. Names like the Somme, Ypres and Flanders are synonymous with the horrors of trench warfare, and the four years of war provided ample opportunity for acts of heroism. A visit to the Somerset Light Infantry Museum at Taunton Castle reveals a number of Victoria Crosses, but many have no Somerset connection other than that the recipients were in the county regiment. There are five men however, who as well as winning the Victoria Cross, can truly claim to be men of Somerset.

Wilfred Dolby Fuller, VC

The first Somerset-born winner of the Victoria Cross in the First World War was Lance Corporal William Fuller of the Grenadier Guards. Fuller was alone in the trenches at Neuve Chapelle in March 1915 when he saw a party of the enemy trying to move along a communication trench. Without hesitation, he ran towards them and killed the leading German with a grenade. The impact on the remainder was considerable. Faced by such a determined foe and with nowhere to go to evade yet more grenades, the group of fifty surrendered themselves to Fuller despite outnumbering him fifty to one. For this action he received the Victoria Cross. He died in Frome in November 1947 aged 54 and is buried there in Christchurch churchyard.

Oliver Brooks, VC

Oliver Brooks was born in Midsomer Norton in 1889. He joined the army as a sixteen year old lad, serving at home and in the Reserves before being recalled to the colours and sent to France when war broke out in 1914. The Christmas of 1914 is often quoted as a period of sanity in an otherwise insane war. Stories are told of how in some sectors soldiers declared their own truce on Christmas Day and troops from opposing trenches played football. Elsewhere the war continued, and Oliver Brooks spent the day throwing grenades into German trenches.

By July 1915 he was a Lance Sergeant in the Coldstream Guards. Three months later he was at Loos in northern France where his battalion was attempting to capture two hundred yards of territory. The enemy had been shelling it relentlessly, but Oliver Brooks led his platoon with such determination that the stretch was successfully captured despite the hail of shells to which his men were exposed. His reward was the Victoria Cross, which was presented to him by George V in the hospital train in which the King was recovering after falling from his horse whilst visiting the troops.

On retiring from the army, Sergeant Brooks worked for many years as a doorman, including a spell at the Dorchester Hotel in London. He died in October 1940.

Reverend Edward Noel Mellish, VC

The London-born Reverend Edward Mellish adopted Somerset as his home when he retired to the village of South Petherton. His claim to fame is that he was the first member of the army's chaplaincy to be awarded the Victoria Cross.

Having taken holy orders in 1912, he began his military service in 1915. In late March of the following year, he was serving as chaplain to the 4th Battalion of the Royal Fusiliers. They were at a road junction near St Eloi in Belgium, which the Germans controlled from the surrounding high ground. Heavily defended with barbed wire and manned with machine gun positions, it formed part of an impenetrable front some six hundred yards long. A concerted effort was called for if a breakthrough was to be achieved.

A number of tunnelling companies had dug tunnels beneath the enemy positions. Six mines were put in place and in the early hours of a March morning they were exploded. With this, two battalions of Fusiliers went over the top to face overwhelming machine gun, rifle and artillery fire. Despite the German resistance, the Fusiliers managed to reach and capture the first German trench position where, weakened in numbers, they had to stop their advance to consolidate their new position.

Scores of men lay wounded, continually raked by machine gun fire. It was no good sending out stretchers under such conditions. All the stretcher bearers could do was to wait and hope that the enemy fire slackened. The Reverend Mellish, however, realised that many of the wounded would not survive if left out there exposed for too long and so he took it on himself to bring back as many as he could. On the first day alone he brought back ten wounded men whilst being swept with machine gun fire. On the second day he brought back twelve more and on the third managed to recruit volunteers to join him in bringing in the remainder. In those first two days the enemy guns and artillery rarely ceased, even when he was walking towards his casualties with his prayer book under his arm as though on his way to church parade.

The respect he earned in those few days was extraordinary. Not even the ambulance men went out in such conditions. One committed Cockney atheist who was rescued by the chaplain apparently, whilst lying in hospital, asked what religion the reverend gentleman was and, when informed, declared that as far as he was concerned he was now that religion as well and anybody who said anything against his church would ''ave 'is bleeding 'ead bashed in!'

The continuous sequence of courageous acts performed by Edward Mellish during those three days in particular earned him the Victoria Cross. In his retirement he settled in South Petherton and it was there that he died in 1962 aged eighty two.

Arthur Hugh Henry Batten-Pooll, VC

In St Lawrence's churchyard, in the village of Woolverton near Frome, can be found the grave of Arthur Batten-Pooll who died in 1971. Arthur is the fourth First World War holder of the Victoria Cross with a Somerset link, which he won in 1916 when serving as a lieutenant near Colonne in France. He was leading a raiding party on the German lines lines when an exploding bomb left him severely wounded. His right hand had been mutilated by the blast, but in spite of the pain, he continued in command and maintained the attack, showing unflinching courage. After half an hour of intense fighting, he was forced to withdraw. Whilst helping to rescue the wounded he was hit again, receiving two further wounds. Declining assistance, the need of others being greater, he made his own way back the hundred yards to the allied lines, where he finally passed out.

John Collins, VC

Not all the action in First World War was on the Western Front. It was in Palestine that John Collins, who was born at West Hatch in Somerset, was to win his Victoria Cross in October 1917. In similar fashion to the Reverend Mellish, Corporal Collins repeatedly went out under heavy enemy fire to bring back the wounded. In a later action he led an assault over uncut wire and under heavy close fire. Having killed fifteen of the enemy, he took a Lewis gun section and, despite being under sniper fire and isolated from his group, organised the consolidation of the troops. His Victoria Cross can be found in the Royal Welch Fusiliers' Museum in Caernarfon Castle.

Francis Foley – Somerset's Schindler

Somerset's Highbridge born Francis Foley provides a convenient link between the First and Second World Wars. As a young man, he escaped from Germany at the start of the Great War, in disguise and on foot. Then in the Second World War, he was responsible for saving more than ten thousand Jews from the Holocaust. But let's begin his story in Israel.

Just outside Jerusalem is a plantation of trees and a plaque reading, 'Major Francis Edward Foley, England, Memorial Grove'. On a June day in 1959, a small but select group of people gathered at the grove. Over two thousand trees had already been planted and each day money for more was still pouring in. The cost of each tree had been met by someone who had been saved from almost certain death in the concentration camps of Germany by the kindness of just one man, Francis Edward Foley. Described as 'The man who saved ten thousand Jews', a label which many believe well understates the total number of people he saved, Francis Foley was being honoured at long last. Benno Cohn declared that, 'Day and night, he was at the disposal of those who sought help. In those dark days, he restored to many of us our faith in humanity'.

What the memorial doesn't tell us is the enormous risk that Foley took in saving all those lives. For months at a time he was operating undercover under the noses of the German Gestapo. If captured, this humble son of Somerset would have been shot as a spy. For many years, his story was untold, until the writer Michael Smith published *Foley: The Spy who Saved 10,000 Jews*. The book which resulted from his research was sufficient to convince the Yad Vashem Holocaust Museum that Foley deserved to be recognised with the title of 'Righteous Among the Nations', the highest honour the Jewish nation can award to a non-Jew and one which is not awarded lightly. Amongst previous recipients were Oskar Schindler and Raoul Wallenberg.

Highbridge

Francis Foley – known as Frank – was born in 1884 at 7 Walrow Terrace in Highbridge. His father Andrew worked for the Somerset and Dorset Joint Railway Company, and the family's simple two-up two-down terrace home was near the railway station. There Frank and his three brothers and a sister lived with their mother Isabel.

Isabel was a Roman Catholic and the children all attended the local Catholic school in neighbouring Burnham-on-Sea. For some reason, Foley was transferred at the age of nine to the St John's Church of England School in Highbridge. At the time, he had ambitions to become a priest. His sister Margaret did in fact later become a nun. He later went to a Jesuit school in Lancaster and then, aged eighteen, to the Catholic St. Joseph's College in Poitiers, France. Three further years were spent in Poitiers University before he abandoned the idea of the priesthood and travelled Europe, working in Austria, Holland, Denmark and Germany.

Escape from Germany

In August 1914, Frank was in Hamburg studying philosophy when the Great War broke out. He was already fluent in German and French and he knew that the Germans were rounding up British citizens for internment. He had to escape the country before being identified. He borrowed a Prussian officer's uniform and set off by train towards

Frisia where he hoped to cross the border into northern Holland. Leaving the train at Bremen, he exchanged his army uniform for civilian clothes and continued on foot. It took many days to complete the journey to the port of Emden where a priest put him in touch with a fisherman who gave him safe passage to Holland.

Foley knew that if he was caught, he would be shot as a spy. Several foreigners had already been captured and lynched as a result of the spy fever running rampant throughout Germany. Undoubtedly this experience gave Foley a genuine feeling for what it was like to be hunted and to live in fear for one's life.

On reaching England, he returned to Somerset and his parents' new home in the centre of Burnham. He temporarily took a teaching job in a preparatory school prior to enlisting into the army. Time spent in the Officer Training Corps was followed by a commission as a second lieutenant and at the start of 1917 he was dispatched to France. By the time he was finally posted to the Somme, Foley had been promoted and saw considerable action. In just one massive German attack, six hundred of the men around him were killed or listed as missing, presumed dead. It had been an horrific experience and one which left Foley questioning his faith. Evacuated to England for treatment, it was discovered that his left lung had been damaged by a German bullet, leaving him with breathing difficulties. His days in uniform were over.

MI6

As one door closed, so another one opened. Someone in the War Office had noticed that Foley had been 'mentioned in dispatches' and that he had language skills. They were also aware of his daring escape from Germany. He appeared to have all the characteristics and knowledge the Secret Service required.

Captain Foley joined MI6, where he learnt how to recruit agents, how to run a network, how to code messages. One of his first postings was to a brothel behind enemy lines from where he observed and reported on railway movements. One technique for reporting troop numbers was to publish a knitting pattern in a magazine, using plain stitches to indicate troops and pearl to indicate horses.

In the post-war era, Foley was appointed to head the Passport Control Office in Berlin. This had a two fold purpose. Anyone wishing to enter Britain or any of the Empire countries had to be vetted at their nearest British Passport Control Office. This gave the authorities a chance to check on any subversive activity. But more importantly, it gave Foley a cover for his real role as the head of a spy ring. He effectively had two jobs, the second of which would be denied by his employers if he were ever caught. But it was a fascinating task, taking him on frequent visits to the infamous Berlin nightclubs then at the heart of any subversive activity in the city. In between, he still found time for trips home to Burnham and to find a wife, Kay, who, in 1921, travelled with him back to Berlin after their wedding.

Escape visas

Foley served in the dual role of passport officer and spymaster throughout the 1930's when Hitler was rising to power. Mistrust of the Jews turned gradually to presecution. Jews in increasing numbers were attempting to leave Germany, but increasingly it was being made impossible for them to do so. Before any hope of escape was possible they needed visas for entry into another country. Back in Britain, anti-Jewish feeling was also growing. The official line was to refuse requests from Jews to enter Britain. A London magistrate when sentencing three Jews to imprisonment for entering England without visas declared, 'It's an outrage how Jews are pouring into the country'. But meanwhile in Berlin, Foley was handing out travel documents to the long queues who gathered outside his office on a daily basis from all parts of Germany. For those thousands of people, it was a matter of life or death.

As well as working fourteen hours a day, Foley was defying the official instructions from his masters and risking his job in so doing. For those unable to evade Nazi persecution, he helped by planning and executing their escape from Germany using the escape channel specifically set up by Foley for himself and his wife should the time come, even providing forged passports where necessary. He had no diplomatic immunity and ran the serious risk of being shot if discovered. He even drove to the concentration camps armed with travel documents for those for who could not get them prior to being rounded up. At the gates of the camps he demanded their release. Dozens were hidden overnight in his home, which meant that Kay was also at risk.

Vital intelligence

Many of the Jews he helped in return provided him with vital information regarding Nazi activity. The wife of one man arrested by the Germans appealed to Foley for help. Without hesitation, he forged papers for her and her children to get them out of Germany. He then went to the Gestapo headquarters brandishing the paperwork for the husband and demanded his release. That night the family flew out to Holland. It was dangerous ground on which he was treading. He even helped a member of the Nazi party arrange the escape of his Jewish wife and their daughter.

As the war clouds gathered, the panic to leave Germany intensified. Kay was now also working alongside her husband in an attempt to stem the tide of paperwork. The queue outside of his office was as much as a mile long. Many in it were crying and hysterical, desperate for help in escaping Germany before the concentration camps claimed them as their victims. He arranged for a tea trolley to serve the long line waiting in the biting chill outside. Put quite simply, Frank Foley's ability to provide the required paperwork was the difference between life and death.

His task became increasingly dangerous, the risk of capture was heightened. On more than one occasion, Nazi agents arrived at his office to observe what was going on. Foley dealt with them by asking if they were applying for visas, in which case they should join the end of the queue like everyone else. When they answered that they were not, he instructed them to leave the office. It wasn't just the office where he was at risk. It was only a matter of time before someone questioned why so many Jews were arriving at Foley's Berlin home at three or four in the morning.

In August 1939, Kay and Francis Foley were obliged to pull out of Berlin as Britain positioned itself to declare war on Germany. A week later the two nations were officially at war. The exact number of people he saved from the camps in this way will never be known, but Hubert Pollack, one of Foley's Secret Service agents, has confirmed that, without exaggeration, over a six year period, tens of thousands more received visas than would otherwise have been the case.

So how do the actions of Frank Foley compare with the likes of Oskar Schindler and Raoul Wallenberg? As noble as Schindler's actions were, his business benefited from the Jewish labour that he saved and in terms of numbers, they were a fraction of those saved by Foley. Wallenberg, on the other hand, operated under diplomatic immunity and was never at risk of his life. For Foley there was no commercial benefit, only the risk of execution if caught, and no diplomatic immunity. So why has his name not enjoyed the fame of the other two? Perhaps because Foley was simply a modest man. Perhaps because to reveal his story may have exposed others whose undercover work still continued.

Foley's work continued throughout the war. His team uncovered scores of German spies, some of whom he recruited as double agents. He persuaded German scientists not to reveal their information and knowledge in respect of atomic weapons and rockets. He even organised the operation which saved the Norwegian gold reserves from falling into German hands. As the end of the war approached, he was the principle negotiator with Rudolph Hess when Hess flew to Britain to try to negotiate a peace deal.

When the war was over, Foley and his spy network turned their attention to Russia, at least until his retirement. Francis Foley died of a heart attack in 1953 aged 78. His home town of Burnham-on-Sea now boasts a road bearing his name.

War comes to Somerset

Whilst most of the action of the Second World War took place overseas, at home the population lived in fear of German air raids. Right from the opening weeks of the war, bombs fell on Somerset, mostly in remote areas, but at times the damage was considerable.

Lieutenant Reynolds, George Medal
One such bomb fell into the garden of a house in Congresbury where it failed to explode. Lieutenant Reynolds from the Royal Engineers was called in to see to its disposal. The problem was its inaccessible position, twenty five feet below ground. Reynolds was lowered head first into the hole where, operating upside down, he removed three fuses. One was a timer which he defused with just half an hour to spare. Reynolds was awarded the George Medal.

Other bomb disposal men were not so lucky. In Yeovil three members of a bomb disposal team were killed when the bomb they were attempting to defuse, twenty feet down a shaft, exploded.

Raids over Bristol were frequent but Somerset's largest centre of population, Bath, had been left pretty well unscathed until two successive nights in April 1942. Known as the Baedeker raids, and carried out by groups of forty or fifty bombers at a time, the city was devastated by an onslaught of high explosive bombs and incendiaries. Hundreds of civilians were killed. It was a time for heroes, and there were many during those two nights and the days that followed.

It was just after eleven at night when the bombing began. The German planes just kept circling and dropping their payloads. Whilst nearby Bristol was reasonably defended, Bath was less able to defend itself. The bombers were able to fly in low with little threat of being shot down. It was a moonlit night and the additional light from flares and incendiaries made targeting the city much easier. No sooner had phone calls started to pour in reporting the need for emergency services, when the communications centre for the city was hit and it became necessary to carry all messages using dispatch riders, who ran the gauntlet of falling bombs and flying masonry.

At one of the city's casualty service depots a pregnant lady, Mrs. J. M. Woolmer, was manning the phones. She remained at her post right through the crisis despite the fact that in the same room was an unexploded bomb which had crashed through the roof and come to rest on a bed. Mrs. Woolmer was awarded the British Empire Medal.

Corporal E. E. Webb, King's Commendation for Brave Conduct.
The Stothert and Pitt engineering works was one of the targets in Bath hit by the Germans. Corporal E. E. Webb had left his home at around half past eleven to report for duty at the factory, which made tank turrets and mini submarines, but on his way he stopped at the top of Shaftesbury Road where a house had been demolished by a bomb and a man was trapped inside. He helped a police officer free and carry the man out of the building and then in Lower Oldfield Park he rescued two elderly ladies from a collapsing house. Further down the same road, it was discovered that eight people were trapped in a house. The premises next door were already ablaze and it was only a matter of time before those inside perished.

A hole was punched in the wall, through which Corporal Webb crawled to where the residents were trapped in a basement slowly filling up with smoke. A saw was passed to him and, one by one, over an hour working in the hot, smoky and dangerous building, he freed each of the eight. He was awarded the King's Commendation for Brave Conduct.

Sergeant B. Brown, MM

Sergeant Brown was passing close to a building in Bath at the very moment it was struck by a bomb. With no hesitation, he ran in to find a man trapped beneath some fallen timbers and rubble. The task of extricating him was dangerous as the building was likely to collapse. Heedless of the risk, he helped the man to safety and then returned to rescue three ladies, similarly trapped. The building later collapsed, and for his quick-thinking and courage Sergeant Brown was awarded the Military Medal. He was a member of the Home Guard, the 5th Somerset (Bath City) Battalion, and was one of the lucky survivors. Nine of the battalion were killed during the raids, and many others wounded.

Company Sergeant-Major J. A. Leslie, GM

Bath also had a 6th Somerset Battalion which was attached to the Admiralty. They also were fully stretched throughout the Baedeker raids and many were witness to the terrible damage done on the second night to the Regina Hotel, opposite the Assembly Rooms in Bennett Street. Privates Baker, Martell and Rees with Company Sergeant-Major Leslie, all from the 6th Somerset Battalion, were to distinguish themselves.

The hotel had been badly hit and despite the fact that the air raid was still in full flow, many of its guests were trapped inside. The four men entered the burning building. Once inside Leslie crawled into the basement through a small hole. There he found a woman hanging upside down from her knees and trapped by the falling masonry. Leslie supported her while the other members of his team struggled to free her. So concerned were they that the entire hotel might fall on them, they put up a sheet to hide them from the full horror of their probable fate.

There was also a great risk of fire and several times Leslie had to be doused with water to stop his clothes from catching alight. His courage earned him the George Medal and the King's Commendation for Bravery. The woman was rescued thanks to their valiant efforts but there was no respite. In total they brought out twenty five bodies, only five of those alive. Later that night Leslie scrambled up the side of a building to tear down burning shop blinds to prevent a fire from spreading.

Privates N. W. S. Baker, BEM; J. M. Martell, BEM; H. D. Rees, BEM

His three colleagues, all privates, were also relentless in the endeavours. Private Baker spent a total of four and a half hours in the basement helping free and rescue those trapped. Later he went upstairs, rescuing two more guests despite the risk of the hotel's imminent collapse. Private Martell meanwhile had forced another hole into the basement and, with just a torch to provide him with light, dragged more people from the burning building. Private Rees likewise had been involved from the start of the rescue, remaining on duty from early morning on the day of the raid until the evening of the following day; 36 hours without taking a break. His efforts helped in the rescue of twenty five people of whom tragically only five survived. All three of the privates received the British Empire Medal.

When the raids were over and the dust settled, the damage was assessed. 417 people had been killed and over a thousand buildings completely destroyed. For Bath, the worst at least was over.

Corporal Frederick Alfred Duke, BEM

Stories of individual heroism were repeated all over Somerset. In January 1943 a Wellington bomber crashed near the airbase at Yeovilton. A member of the Home Guard, Corporal Frederick Duke, was off duty when he heard the aircraft struggling to make a forced landing and witnessed the explosion and crash which followed. Jumping from his bike, he raced towards the plane and was thrown to the ground from the impact of another explosion. Whilst common sense dictated a diplomatic withdrawal, he heard screams from the rear gunner's turret and continued towards the aircraft which was now burning fiercely; further explosions were likely.

Reaching the rear gunner's turret, Duke could see a young airman trapped inside. To help him get out, Dukes caught hold of the machine gun projecting through the turret and swung the turret around, badly burning his hands. A serviceman from the nearby air station and a farmer arrived to give a hand. Machine gun ammunition was exploding in the heat and flames added to the danger. None of the rescuers knew if the bomber was carrying any bombs, which potentially could have killed them all instantly.

Between them they dragged out the airman. Duke had already pulled off a blazing boot from the airman, further burning his hands. As they dragged him away, more explosions shattered the aircraft. As all concerned hit the ground, Duke threw himself across the head of the airman to offer him greater protection. He then returned to the aircraft to see if there were others he could help, but soon realised that no one could survive in the burning wreckage. For his outstanding courage he was awarded the British Empire Medal.

H. J. Pollard, T. J. Cook and J. Ridler – King's Commendation for Bravery

In June 1943, a similar daring rescue took place and three West Somerset men earned the King's Commendation for Bravery. A Halifax bomber had crashed into a combe at Porlock Weir and landed in the woods on the steep hillside. It wasn't long before three local men, H. J. Pollard, J. Cook and J. Ridler, arrived on the scene. Petrol vapour filled the air, making breathing difficult and adding to the dangers. Despite the hazards, Cook and Pollard dragged one airman free and brought out the body of another. Then, without warning, the petrol exploded and blew both men down the hillside. Ridler meanwhile, working with his sleeves rolled up in the heat, received burns so severe he was to spend the next month in hospital. Despite the pain, his first thoughts were with the airman, who he helped get down the hill to safety.

Herbert Wallace Le Patourel, VC

Although his link with Somerset is somewhat tenuous, I include Herbert Le Patourel for reasons of completeness since he was residing in Chewton Mendip at the time of his death. He was born in Guernsey in 1916 and was working in banking when the war broke out. In December 1942 he was a major serving with the Royal Hampshire Regiment at Teboura in Tunisia where his company was under heavy fire. A single machine gun position on high ground was pinning them down and doing untold damage. He personally led a group of four volunteers in an assault on the enemy position. When each of his men lay dead or wounded he continued alone with just pistol and grenades. Finally he was wounded and taken prisoner. The award of the Victoria Cross was made posthumously, the authorities assuming that he had been killed in the action. However, at the time he was recovering in a military hospital in Naples. After being repatriated in 1943 he returned to active service. He died in September 1979 at Chewton Mendip.

Ron Authers – The Bridge on the River Kwai

I first met Ron Authers whilst working at the Courtauld's owned British Cellophane plant in Bridgwater, where Ron served as a security officer. There was something in his air that suggested a military background, but his politeness and quiet confidence gave no clue to the horrifying conditions he had experienced as a prisoner of war in the Far East, as one of those who survived the Railway of Death and the Bridge on the River Kwai.

Across the county there are numerous Somerset men who had similar experience and showed equal courage. Overwhelmingly they are reluctant to talk about those times, such were the horrors they witnessed. I have chosen to relate the experiences of just one, Ron Authers, as an example of many stories which in the main will never be told, but which we should never be allowed to forget.

Ron joined the Royal Engineers, where he specialised in bomb disposal. In 1936 he headed off to the Far East unaware that he would not return home again until November 1945. Three years later, war broke out. By January 1942 the Japanese had joined in and had captured Hong Kong, Borneo, New Guinea and the Solomon Islands. Singapore, still held by the British as a strategically critical point in the Far East, now became the subject of daylight bombing raids.

Japanese advance on Singapore
Weeks of intense fighting followed with no respite and no support from outside. Relentlessly the Japanese advanced. Whole regiments of allied troops were overwhelmed, including British, Indians and Gurkhas. Memories of Dunkirk kept a spark of hope alive that there might be an evacuation. Tragically the only news to come through was

Lord Wavell's order to fight on to the last bullet.

Ron and his unit dug in at Singapore. Shelled from all sides and ceaselessly blanket bombed from the air, the end must have appeared inevitable. They fought day and night, the artillery sleeping by their guns. The city was ablaze. Burning fuel created a river of fire as it followed the main water course through the city centre.

The nurses from the hospital were evacuated by boat to the island of Java. There, captured by the Japanese, they were made to wade back into the sea where they were machine gunned to death. This was a taste of the cruelty yet to come.

The Fall of Singapore

In February 1942 Singapore finally fell after twelve weeks of bitter but increasingly hopeless fighting. Ron and his fellow survivors, now prisoners of the Japanese, had heard the tales of Japanese atrocities in China but equally knew that Japan had signed up to the Geneva Convention. They could only hope they would be honoured as soldiers and treated fairly.

Ron and his fellow prisoners of war, defeated and dejected, marched through the streets of Singapore. Devastation surrounded them. Rotting corpses lay in drains, hung from the backs of trucks or lay in the doorways where they had fallen, flies swarming in the stench of decay. It was a pleasure to leave the city behind and breathe in the fresh country air as they marched to Changi Prison in a suburb of Singapore.

Initially Changi seemed pleasant enough. Having been a British Army billet, it was clean and dry. The first few weeks were spent burying bodies, including hundreds of Chinese civilians who had been tied together in groups with barbed wire before being shot and left to rot on the beach. But the days of relatively comfortable living were soon over.

The first sign was a change in their diet. The three square meals a day were replaced by a meagre supply of low grade rice and poor quality vegetables, with a morsel of meat just once a week. Those in hospital had rice water and peanuts. In the weeks that followed, dysentery and skin sores ran through the camp and the prisoners typically lost a third of their body weight.

In May 1942, the Japanese moved the entire camp to Selerang

Barracks, where the men were crammed in with just half a square foot of sleeping space per man. The queues for beds were equalled by those for the latrines. In October Ron was moved to Thailand. Herded with the others into railway trucks, they sweltered in the heat for the next five days as the train rumbled westward. Those that died were buried at the wayside whenever the train stopped. A few took advantage to effect their escape but were heard of no more.

The Railway of Death

Ron and his comrades wondered what lay ahead. An enquiry from a British officer established that their destination was a work camp. Those unable to work would be shot. It was as blunt as that. Their journey finally reached the end of the railway. From here on, they would trek on foot through the jungle.

That evening they commenced the march along the route which would become the 'Railway of Death'. To build the railway, the jungle first had to be cleared – a task that claimed hundreds of lives. Shelters were built from palm fronds and ground sheets. Sleep meant lying in inches of water and mud. After a few days, they embarked on an even tougher march to their next camp. There was no road, just a waterlogged trail. Day after day, prisoners fell dead by the wayside. Still Ron marched on, ever weakening, but it was only those with the strongest wills who were to survive the coming ordeals.

On Guy Fawkes Day they arrived at the camp at Kanu. Once there, weeks of breaking rocks and cutting timbers followed as work began on the railway which was to form a link between Singapore and Burma.

Crushed by an elephant

With the prolonged hours of hard labour and the totally inadequate diet, now typically half a litre of rice a day, their numbers continued to dwindle. In their emaciated state, four men at a time were expected to lift and carry logs which otherwise an elephant alone would carry. On one such occasion, Ron found himself crushed between an elephant and a tree. The accident left him with an injury to his back that was to plague him for the rest of his life.

Day after day, they were driven out of their huts and forced to march along the mud trails to the railway site. There they worked day and night before dragging themselves back to the camp. Those that faltered were beaten, bayoneted or shot.

During this time, no news filtered through from the outside world. No one in the camps was aware that the tide was gradually turning against the Japanese. Despite their ignorance, they did their best to find ways to help the war effort. Ron and his fellow prisoners placed termites in the timbers of the bridges they were building in the hope that the insects would cause them to weaken and rot. This act was to haunt them when, eighteen months later, they travelled by train back over the same bridges, destined for Singapore, uncertain as to whether or not the bridges would collapse.

Wam Poh cutting

Whilst excavating a huge cutting into a cliff face at Wam Poh, Ron saw a fellow prisoner fall into the river below. The Japanese allowed no one to go to his aid, and for five days Ron watched his friend slowly die in the shallow water below.

As the prisoners cut their way through rocks and undergrowth, they frequently uncovered the skeletons of their comrades who had fallen earlier, now devoid of all flesh thanks to the ravages of the local ants. But these forays into the undergrowth provided the chance for an occasional meal of reptile, rodent or wild bird. These were the only real source of protein in their diet.

This was a time when friendship meant a great deal, when the efforts of their fellow prisoners kept some from those total depths of despair from which there is no return. Crammed into tents, with six men to a six by four foot bamboo bed, high degrees of tolerance and understanding were required. One companion of Ron's was Ronald Searle, the author of the famous St. Trinian stories, who shared the bed next to him and vividly recounts this period in his memoirs.

The Bridge on the River Kwai

The time came for Ron and hundreds of others to move further up country to build what was to become the infamous Bridge on the River Kwai. A four mile march in each direction, along roads knee deep with mud, came at either end of an eight hour shift on the bridge. Again the weak simply fell by the wayside.

Cholera struck the camps and hundreds died each night. Those that

ABOVE Lieutenant Neville Howse (1863-1930) of Stogursey carrying a wounded bugler to safety when serving in the Army Medical Corps during the Boer War, an action that earned him the Victoria Cross.

Howse was later knighted after becoming the first head of the Australian Army Medical Service.

LEFT Wilfred Fuller, VC, on duty as a police officer at Taunton Police Station. Fuller was the first Somerset-born winner of the Victoria Cross in the First World War, which he won when serving with the Grenadier Guards at Neuve Chapelle in 1915. He died in Frome in 1947, and lies buried in Christchurch churchyard.

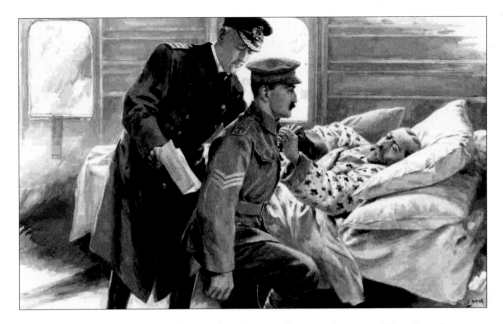

ABOVE An illustration from the *London Gazette* showing Sergeant Oliver Brooks (1889-1940) of Midsomer Norton receiving his Victoria Cross from King George V in 1915.

BELOW Corporal John Collins (1880-1951) of West Hatch, who won the Victoria Cross whilst serving with the Royal Welch Fusiliers in Palestine in 1917.

Two of Somerset's winners of the Victoria Cross in the First World War were later commemmorated on cigarette cards.

LEFT Lieutenant Arthur Batten-Pooll (1891-1971) who won the Victoria Cross in France in 1916 when serving with the Royal Munster Fusiliers, and is buried in Woolverton churchyard near Frome.

BELOW Captain the Reverend Noel Mellish (1880-1962) retired to South Petherton after winning the Victoria Cross in 1916 whilst serving as a chaplain with the Royal Fusiliers. Over three days, and raked by continuous machine gun fire, Mellish brought back men wounded after an attack on the German trenches. Mellish was the first member of the army's chaplaincy to be awarded the Victoria Cross. He is buried in Weymouth Crematorium.

Frank Foley (1884-1953) was born at Highbridge and died at Burnham-on-Sea, where a street now bears his name. After serving in France during the First World War, Foley joined MI6. As head of the British Passport Office in Berlin he risked his life to help thousands of Jews escape from Nazi Germany. In reviewing Michael Smith's book on Foley, *Foley, The Spy who Saved 10,000 Jews,* the *Daily Mail* described his story as 'one of the greatest untold stories of heroism and humanity from the Second World War.'

The Regina Hotel, Bath, after the Baedeker raid of April 27 1942. The courage of Sergeant-Major J.A. Leslie and Privates N.W.S. Baker, J.M. Martell and H.D. Rees of the 6th Somerset (Bath Admiralty) Battalion of the Home Guard in rescuing men and women trapped inside the burning building resulted in the award of the George Medal to Sergeant-Major Leslie and the British Empire Medal to the three privates.

Ron Authers of the Royal Engineers safely back home in England after surviving imprisonment by the Japanese in Changi after the surrender of Singapore in 1942, followed by working in appalling conditions on both the 'Railway of Death' and the Bridge on the River Kwai.

Herbert Le Patourel (1916-1979) of the Royal Hampshire Regiment who won the Victoria Cross whilst serving in North Africa in 1942. He died at Chewton Mendip and is buried in South Bristol Crematorium.

Assistant Surgeon Campbell Douglas (1840-1909) of the 24th Regiment (later the South Wales Borderers) who won his Victoria Cross fighting islanders in the Bay of Bengal in 1867.

RIGHT Lieutenant George Lewis Browne
(1784-1856) who served under Nelson at
Trafalgar on H.M.S. *Victory*, later
retiring as a Captain to Bridgwater.

BELOW Lieutenant Commander
Gerard Roope (1905-1940) who
died when commanding H.M.S.
Glowworm off Norway in 1940.
The posthumous award of the
Victoria Cross to Roope for
ramming the German cruiser
Admiral Von Hipper marks the only
occasion when such an award has
been granted on the recommendation
of the enemy – in this case the captain
of the *Hipper*.

survived laboured on, wracked with pain. Sick and wounded, they toiled away each day, determined to survive. These men were experiencing one of the most appalling examples of ill-treatment that one nation has ever inflicted on another. One respite was the occasional soak in a nearby river where a species of small fish sucked the pus from their ulcers and sores. Inexplicably these small fish appeared to have a healing effect on the wounds and their attention was most welcome.

Back to Singapore

For Ron, and many others, the suffering on the Railway of Death and the Bridge on the River Kwai came to an end in June 1943 when he was moved back to Singapore. On the return journey, the fittest of the group were detailed each day to remove the corpses of those who had died since the last halt. Even the fittest now resembled skeletons.

In a transit camp on the route to Singapore, conditions were much better. British medical officers tended the sick. Wounds were dressed daily and there was plenty of rest. Those that survived were eventually rounded up into trucks to complete the journey to Singapore. After an initial delousing, life settled down to a more relaxed pace, with much better food for the next couple of months. Gradually Ron put on weight as did the others, but their bodies, in their weakened state, were prone to every rash and ailment that came along.

Torpedoed and sunk

In early September, Ron left Singapore on a ship bound for Japan where he was to be part of the forced labour in a Mitsubishi factory. But if Ron thought life could only improve, he had a rude awakening. Their ship was in collision with another at sea, and then on the following day was torpedoed by an American submarine, unaware of the Allied POW's on board. Ron and a fellow POW spent the next two days and nights clinging naked to a piece of timber. As the hours passed on the second day, and their physical state deteriorated, they knew that should darkness fall, neither would survive another night in the water. A pact was agreed that once darkness fell, they would let go the piece of timber, and quietly sink together.

With probably no more than ten minutes to go before darkness fell, they were rescued by a Japanese tanker, only to be taken on board and flogged in front of the crew. Transferred to a whaler the following day, they finally completed their journey to Japan. The next nine months were spent labouring for the Mitsubishi company at Nagasaki. During that time Ron saw the first incendiaries fall on Japan, a sign that the Japanese were not having it all there own way. There was still hope.

Hiroshima and Nagasaki
Then on 9 August, 1945 Ron witnessed the atom bomb fall on Nagasaki. His first impression was that the allied bombers had hit a huge ammunition dump. The day after, he was accidentally dive-bombed and machine-gunned by the Americans, making him wonder if the Americans would succeed in finishing him off where the Japanese had thus far failed!

A week later, Emperor Hirohito surrendered. Perhaps for the first time, Ron could contemplate a return to England with renewed optimism, born from a confusion of hope and despair. The voyage home was via Honolulu, San Francisco, Vancouver and New York aboard the *Queen Mary*, which docked in Southampton in November 1945. It was the first time he had set foot on English soil since his departure with the Royal Engineers nine years earlier.

Ron stayed in the army until 1957 when he took up employment as a security officer at the Cellophane plant in Bridgwater, where he remained until his retirement. After a full and active life, and one in which he had seen more than most of us would care to consider, Ron passed away in 1990. He was laid to rest in St. Mary's churchyard in Bridgwater, just one unsung hero among many.

FIVE

The Cruel Sea

The sea can be a cruel mistress, whether in conflict or peace. In this chapter we combine wartime bravery with dramatic rescues along the Somerset coast during times of peace.

Captain George Lewis Browne
The Battle of Trafalgar

Early days

George Lewis Browne was born in Bridgwater in 1784. To escape being bullied whilst at the local grammar school, he climbed the rigging of shipping along the quayside, fostering his love of ships and the sea. Aged thirteen. he entered the navy to train as a midshipman.

These were the years of Napoleon and the French Revolutionary Wars. In 1801 he caught the attention of Captain Thomas Hardy, and soon came under his command. Together they sailed to the West Indies and, when Hardy was given command of the *Victory* in 1803 following the outbreak of war with France, Midshipman Browne went with him.

HMS *Victory*

It was on board the *Victory* that Browne earned Nelson's praise and admiration. 'I assure you,' he wrote, 'that I most sincerely wish to promote Browne, who is an ornament to our service; but alas! Nobody will be so good as to die, nor will the French kill us. What can I do? - but I live in hopes,'

But Nelson soon had his way, presenting Browne with his lieutenant's commission on the quarter deck of the *Victory* on August 1 1804, the anniversary of the Battle of the Nile, when Browne was still only twenty.

First command

Nelson gave Browne command of the *Buona Ventura*, a captured Spanish ship. With a small force, Browne sailed the Barcelona coast and captured a Spanish prize, taking with it a sizeable crew and valuable cargo. Nelson recalled him to the *Victory*, where, to quote from his obituary, 'Lieutenant Browne distinguished himself by an attention to his professional duties which has never been excelled; for two and a half years scarcely ever setting his foot ashore except when on duty; his leisure hours were always spent in studies connected with his profession, and instructing the youngsters under his care'.

In 1805, the *Victory* sailed for Cadiz, where the French and Spanish fleets were reported to have gathered. The Battle of Trafalgar was in the making. Nelson had under his command twenty seven ships of the line, four frigates, a schooner and a cutter. The French and Spanish had thirty three battleships, outnumbering Nelson, but the British fleet was better disciplined and boasted more powerful guns.

Nelson's signal

Lieutenant Browne was the *Victory*'s assistant signal officer, a post held by a Lieutenant Pasco. Most documents recording the events leading up to the battle state that Nelson requested Pasco to raise the signal that, 'England confides that every man will do his duty'; before adding, 'You must be quick, for I have one more to make, which is for 'Close Action''.

Pasco replied, 'If your lordship will permit me to substitute expects for confides, the signal will soon be completed': the word 'expects' could be sent with a single flag, whereas 'confides' required every letter to be signalled.

'That will do, Pasco,' replied Nelson, 'make it directly'.

And so the signal was hoisted to the masthead, to be welcomed by enthusiastic cheers across the fleet, which gradually faded as the drums called the crews to their stations.

One memoir from another officer on the *Victory* recounts that it was not Pasco but Browne who hoisted the signal. This version gives full credit to Browne as the officer who asked Nelson's approval to change the wording. Credence is given to this by other accounts which report Pasco as sick at the critical time.

In the thick of the action

Irrespective of who should take the credit, no one can belittle Lieutenant Browne's role in the battle. Stationed on the upper deck, he was at the very thickest of the fighting, where the loss of life and risk of being wounded was at its most severe

For twenty minutes, Collingwood, leading one column on the *Royal Sovereign*, engaged the Spanish line, attacking the *Santa Anna,* the flagship. The *Victory* leading the remainder of the fleet was soon to follow and came under immediate attack from the *Neptune*. The *Victory* and the *Temeraire* became locked in close battle with the French *Redoubtable*, broadside after broadside being fired. The close fighting was intense and Lieutenant Browne was in the thick of the action.

Nelson's fatal wound

The fighting had lasted an hour when a French sniper's bullet struck Nelson. Lieutenant Browne could see his admiral, kneeling, mortally wounded on the deck and watched as his old friend, Thomas Hardy, carried him below decks, where he finally died. The battle continued until the combined enemy fleets were defeated. The British lost 449 men killed and 1241 injured; the French and Spanish lost 4,408 killed and 2,545 wounded. Nelson had secured naval supremacy of the seas and with it shattered Napoleon's dreams for his future domination of the nations of Europe.

The triumph of victory was tempered by the loss of Nelson. On his return to England, as the nation mourned, Browne took his place at Nelson's funeral, bearing Nelson's banner rolls and standing at the graveside as the hero's coffin was laid to rest.

The *Victory* was taken out of commission and Browne transferred to the *Ocean* in December 1805 under the flag of Admiral Lord Collingwood, who appointed him flag-lieutenant. Together they sailed to the Mediterranean. Five years later, Collingwood died just two days after requesting Browne's promotion to Commander.

George Browne took responsibility for the safe passage home of Collingwood's body and attended his funeral. He never went to sea again, serving the next thirty years on half pay and accepting the rank of Post Captain on the retired list in 1840.

Return home

During those thirty years, having returned to Bridgwater, an unsuccessful attempt to farm was followed by a period studying law, which finally resulted in his becoming a magistrate. He also served as branch manager for the West of England Bank until declining health forced his retirement.

George Browne died in 1856 and his memorial plaque in Bridgwater's Unitarian Chapel, of which he was an active member, tells how, 'During many years of active service, Captain Browne attained the trust and highest commendation of Admiral Lord Nelson under whose immediate command he distinguished himself at the Battle of Trafalgar. After the restoration of peace, he became a barrister at Law in the Inner Temple and subsequently a magistrate of the County of Somerset.'

Browne and his wife now lay at rest in a family grave in Bridgwater's Wembdon Road cemetery,

Lt. John Bythesea, VC

John Bythesea was the first Somerset man to be awarded the Victoria Cross. He was born in Freshford between Bath and Trowbridge in 1827 and was awarded the VC in 1854 during the Crimean War. He rose to the rank of Rear Admiral, died in 1906, and was laid to rest at Bath Abbey. His medal is now on display at the Royal Naval Museum in Portsmouth.

Throughout the Crimean War, the gathering of intelligence was critical to the successful strategic planning of the campaign. One such opportunity arose when HMS *Arrogant*, a British man-of-war, was engaged in operations in the Baltic Sea just off the coast of Finland. The Russians were active in the area and Russian mail was being carried from island to island under the protection of a guard.

Somerset's twenty-seven-year old Lt. John Bythesea had picked up a local fisherman who told him that mail was being sent from a Russian fortress to the Tsar. Realizing its potential importance, Bythesea persuaded his captain to allow him to go ashore and attempt to intercept the mail and its guard. Expecting scant resistance, he took a stoker called William Johnstone, landed, set up their ambush, and awaited the arrival of the mail.

To their horror, when it finally appeared, it was under the protection of five armed guards. Outnumbered, and with just the one pistol between them, Bythesea and Johnstone captured the mail and three of its guards, returning safely to the ship. John Bythesea and William Johnstone were later awarded the Victoria Cross.

Lieutenant George Fiott Day, VC

In September 1855, Lieutenant George Fiott Day of the Royal Navy, whose grave is in Weston-Super-Mare, won the Victoria Cross whilst serving on HMS *Recruit* in the Crimea.

It was suspected that there were enemy gun positions in the area but their position and strength were unknown. Under cover of darkness, Lt. Day was rowed ashore to reconnoitre the Russian positions and establish whether or not they had any gunboats in the area. Alone and in the dark, he crossed five miles of swamp, at times up to his thighs, with only a pocket compass. At two hundred yards from the Russian naval base, he could see that the gunboats were undermanned, if manned at all, and vulnerable to attack. Returning to the *Recruit*, he reported what he had seen. The following day, gunfire from ashore indicated that the Russian base was no longer so lightly defended. Another mission was needed, for which Day again volunteered.

This time the journey was longer. In pouring rain, Day struggled through several miles of swamp. On reaching the enemy position, he saw that the gunboats were now fully manned and their crews alert and on watch. An attack was now out of the question. Bitterly disappointed, he embarked on the long trek back through the energy sapping swamp. His return journey took so long that the naval party waiting to pick him up gave him up as lost and returned to their ship. Thankfully a fellow officer called Parker was not so easily defeated. Returning to the pick up point, he found Lt. Day lying collapsed and exhausted on the shore. Parker gathered up his fallen colleague and rowed him back to the *Recruit*, where he began his recovery from severe exposure.

George Fiott Day had joined the Royal Navy in 1833 as a First Class Volunteer. During his long career he sailed the world, was wrecked in the chilling waters off the coast of Patagonia in 1835, sweltered in the heat of West Africa in 1837, returning to England in 1838 only to spend the next six and a half years in the Mediterranean. Active service was seen in 1840 during the bombardment of the Syrian coast. In the years that followed he served off the coast of West Africa, at Gunnery School at HMS *Excellent*, the Cape of Good Hope, Brazil, Argentina, the Baltic and back to the Mediterranean and hence to the Black Sea and his Victoria Cross. After further trips to Africa and China, he retired on grounds of ill health in February 1857 having been promoted to Captain.

He moved to Weston-Super-Mare with his wife and daughter in 1875, dying a year later. A headstone was finally unveiled by the Mayor of Weston-Super-Mare on his otherwise unmarked grave in May 2002. His Victoria Cross and other decorations are held in the Sheesh Mahal Museum in Patiala, Punjab, India.

Campbell Mellis Douglas, VC

Canadian born Campbell Douglas lived and died in Wells, where he is buried in the cemetery. In May 1867, he was serving as the assistant surgeon to the 2nd Battalion of the 24th Regiment, later to become the South Wales Borderers. He was one of a group of soldiers who had been sent to Little Andaman Island off the east coast of India in the Bay of Bengal. A British naval party led by a captain had already landed on the island and the entire contingent had disappeared. It was believed they had been killed by cannibalistic islanders.

The ship carrying Campbell Douglas dropped anchor off the island and a scouting party of eighteen was sent ashore. No sooner had they landed then they discovered the remains of the naval captain and his party. Suddenly a violent squall blew up, leaving them stranded on the beach just as the islanders opened fire with bows and arrows from the safety of the jungle. Seeing that his companions were trapped between the sea and arrows, Campbell Douglas took the helm of a small rescue boat and headed for the shore. Time after time he was beaten back by the waves and it was an hour before he finally reached the beach. It took two trips in this fashion to rescue seventeen of the shore party, the eighteenth drowning in the raging surf.

The awarding of the Victoria Cross in this instance was somewhat unusual in that it is normally only awarded in times of war. Later Campbell Douglas was to reach the rank of Lieutenant-Colonel. In his retirement, he continued canoeing, even crossing the English Channel.

Basil Godfrey Place, VC,

Our final name in the list of Somerset's VC's belongs to Basil Place, whose grave can be found in Corton Denham Cemetery. In September 1943 he was serving as a lieutenant in the Royal Navy at Kaafjord off the west coast of German-occupied Norway, commanding a midget submarine. With him, also in command of a midget submarine was Lieutenant Cameron. Between them they carried out a most daring raid on the German Battleship *Turpitz*. The two lieutenants had to travel a thousand miles from their base, negotiate mine fields and nets, avoiding gun positions and listening posts.

Having positioned themselves next to the *Turpitz*, they placed explosive charges beneath the battleship and then embarked on the long and perilous homeward voyage. An hour later, the explosives detonated and blew such a hole in the *Turpitz* that she was out of action for several months. For his daring endeavour, Basil Place was awarded the Victoria Cross. He finally retired as a Rear Admiral and his medal is now on display in the Imperial War Museum in London.

Gerard Broadmead Roope, VC

In April 1940 the Germans invaded Norway and the Royal Navy was involved in many actions at sea during that period. Once again there were countless individual acts of bravery, but in this particular case the most peculiar circumstances applied. For it was on the recommendation of an enemy officer that Lieutenant-Commander Gerard Roope was to be awarded the Victoria Cross.

Gerard Roope was born in Taunton in March 1905. At the time of the incident which earned him his VC, he was serving as captain of HMS *Glowworm*, a 'G' class destroyer. He was a popular officer, much respected by his crew, who affectionately nicknamed him 'Rammer Roope' after he inadvertently rammed a sister ship during a night exercise. The *Glowworm* was at Harwich at the outbreak of war, and in April 1940 sailed for Norwegian waters as part of the escort for the cruiser HMS *Renown*. Their mission was to intercept the anticipated German invasion force.

In early April they were screening a mine laying operation off the Norwegian coast when the *Glowworm* lost a man overboard and Roope was granted permission to turn his ship around to look for the lost sailor. They failed to find him, but by the time the *Glowworm* was on the correct course again, a considerable distance had been put between the destroyer and the rest of the squadron. Early in the morning of the second day, and still trying to make up the lost ground, they spotted a destroyer on the horizon. Asking the destroyer to identify herself, the response came back that she was Swedish.

She was in fact German and soon opened fire on the *Glowworm*. The *Glowworm* responded in like manner but soon a second German destroyer appeared and joined the now one-sided battle. The weather had turned particularly rough and the two German ships were laden with troops. They appeared to turn and run, but Roope realised this was probably a deliberate ploy intended to draw his own ship closer to the main German invasion fleet, against which the *Glowworm* would stand no chance. Nevertheless, Roope gave chase, hoping it might provide information which could be sent back to the rest of the British force regarding the enemy strength and positions.

Emerging from the other side of the storm, the *Glowworm* came face to face with the huge German heavy cruiser *Admiral Von Hipper*, eight times its size. Roope laid down a smoke screen and from within its cover made two torpedo attacks, releasing ten torpedoes in total but missing each time. Meanwhile, the *Glowworm* had sustained considerable damage from the *Hipper* and was now effectively crippled. If his destroyer was going to go down, Roope was determined to inflict the maximum damage possible on the *Hipper*. Ordering the ship to be turned hard to starboard, he aimed her straight at the enemy cruiser. Too late, the German captain realised what was afoot and attempted to steer away, but his much larger ship

74

manoeuvred more slowly. Roope shouted out the command to prepare to 'Stand by to ram'. The *Glowworm* powered into the side of the cruiser with all guns blazing, ripping off a hundred feet of armour plating and damaging the *Hipper's* torpedo tubes.

With engines now in reverse, the *Glowworm* backed off and managed to put a quarter mile between herself and the *Hipper* before she let loose another salvo from her only gun which was still functioning. But her bow was stove in, she was ablaze amidships and had now lost her power. Roope gave the order to abandon ship. The sea cocks were opened and her crew dived into the cold oil-covered stormy waters. As the *Glowworm* sank, her depth charges blew up, adding to the list of fatalities. Gallantly the captain of the *Hipper* spent an hour picking up as many sailors as he could from the waters. Those on board the *Hipper* dropped down ropes and hauled up anyone who could hang on. Captain Roope remained as long as he could in the water, helping his crew to put lifejackets on. When it came to his turn to be rescued, he was half way up the ship's side when he was hit by a huge wave and thrown back into the sea, disappearing forever. Only thirty one of the complement of a hundred and forty nine men survived.

The Germans treated their prisoners with dignity and respect, hailing them and their captain as heroes for the gallant way they had fought. The *Hipper's* captain later sent a message via the International Red Cross recommending the Somerset born Gerard Roope for the Victoria Cross, the only occasion such an award has been granted on the recommendation of the enemy. The citation in the *London Gazette* was only printed at the end of the war, when those taken prisoner were released and were able to bring home the full story of Roope's heroism.

Titanic – Herbert John Pitman

Herbert John Pitman was born at Sutton Montis, near Castle Cary, in November 1877, one of three children of Sarah and Herbert Pitman. His father died when Herbert was two and his mother later remarried. Herbert left home aged seventeen to go to sea, spending three years as an officer under sail and then transferring to steam. By the time he was thirty four, he had served on the Blue Anchor Line, the Shore Line and the White Star Line, the proud owners of the *Titanic*. In March 1912,

Herbert Pitman was transferred from the *Oceanic* to the *Titanic* as its Third Officer.

The *Titanic* was considered to be unsinkable, and so perhaps the warnings of ice were not taken seriously by those on board on that fateful voyage. Herbert had seen notices above the chart room table summarising the recent messages received. One simply referred to 'ice'. Certainly no one anticipated the huge ice flow which had drifted south and into which they were now sailing.

On the evening of 14 April, Herbert was on duty as Officer of the Watch. At 8 p.m. he recorded the ship's position and, having handed over to the Fourth Officer, retired to his bunk. He was half asleep when he heard the crunch and tearing sound of the liner hitting the iceberg. He assumed the noise to be that of the anchor chain running out and idly wondered why they should be stopping in mid-ocean. A quick visit to the deck in his dressing gown provided no clue. He returned to his berth, lit his pipe and dressed to go on deck. It was now approaching his next watch.

As he dressed, the Fourth Officer burst into his cabin with the news that they had hit an iceberg and water was flooding into the mail room. Once on deck, he found seamen preparing the lifeboats for launching, but all appeared calm and under control. No one he spoke to appeared to have seen the iceberg, nor was there any obvious visible damage to the ship, albeit there was some ice on the deck. But below the water line, a different story was unfolding. Some twenty minutes after the impact, Herbert was ordered to inspect the rate at which the water was flooding in. He estimated that there was already twenty four feet of water on board and that it was rising rapidly. Its impact was such that the locks on the apparently water-tight doors had been wrenched off. There was nothing to do but abandon ship.

Herbert went onto the deck to assist in getting the lifeboats away. As no orders had been given to take to the boats, Herbert Pitman and Second Officer Lightoller took the responsibility themselves. Once they had loaded a lifeboat each, Pitman sought the captain's permission to begin lowering. Had he not shown this initiative, the launching of the lifeboats would have been delayed by several minutes, with much greater loss of life. In the panic, both men and women had come forward to board the lifeboat. Herbert insisted that the women and children went first. Nonetheless three men jumped into the boat, landing with such violence that they broke two of the ribs of one of the ladies.

At this stage Herbert was also in the boat, organising its boarding Satisfied it was ready to launch, he climbed out and left a quartermaster in command, convinced his place was with the ship. The First Officer, however, ordered him to get back in. Herbert was to take command of the lifeboat and then assume overall control once the two lifeboats were away. It was only when the lifeboats had been lowered that Herbert saw the iceberg. He ordered them to pull a safe distance away from the *Titanic*.

About an hour later he watched the stern of the doomed liner rise high into the air, then slowly slide inexorably beneath the bitterly cold North Atlantic. He could hear the cries of those in the water. Few would survive in such conditions and Herbert gave the order to row towards the scene of the disaster to pick up survivors. But panic began to break out in the lifeboat. Those on board were convinced that once within reach of those adrift in the water, they would be overwhelmed and another forty lives would be lost. Herbert, in command, felt torn between the shouts of the drowning and the logic of not overloading his boat. His crew held still on their oars. Over the next hour he listened to the cries of drowning men and women, agonisingly unable to help. Slowly the cries diminished until all was quiet. There was nothing more to be done.

Herbert ordered the two lifeboats to be lashed together to ensure they did not drift apart, and they waited in the darkness hoping for a ship to come to their rescue. Some three hours later, they saw the welcome lights of the *Carpathia* coming over the horizon. Their ordeal was over.

It is at times such as these that tough decisions have to be made. For those that make them, the effects on the lives of the individuals that suffer the consequences can haunt them for a lifetime. Nonetheless Herbert continued his career at sea, finally retiring to the small village of Pitcombe, near Bruton. He died in December 1961 and is buried in Pitcombe churchyard, where a black marble headstone marks his grave.

Lifeboats

Somerset lacks some of the dramatic rescue stories that other coastal counties can boast. Perhaps the lack of cliffs and perilous rocks deprives the county of an abundance of heroic rescues at sea. Nonetheless, it has had its moments. The Royal Naval Lifeboat Institute was formed in 1824, and it was just over fifty years later that Watchet was to get the county's first lifeboat, the *Joseph Somes,* a self-righting thirty-three footer rigged for sailing and rowing.

Coxswain Henry Press and crew

Watchet was never the ideal launch site for a lifeboat. The problem was exaggerated at low tide when the heavy boat had to be pulled over the pebbled shoreline by a team of four horses. That was just what happened on a raging night in April 1878, when a north-westerly gale was pounding the Bristol Channel. A Gloucester trow by the name of *Rose* was blown so heavily that her anchor could not hold and she began drifting towards Watchet. Lives were at risk and so the lifeboat was dragged across the beach and launched. With a gale force wind blowing on shore, the crew had to row into high banking waves. By the time they reached the *Rose* she had already grounded and begun breaking up, but her crew had been rescued by the coastguard. Another vessel, the *Olive Branch*, was in similar danger and the *Joseph Somes* was able to go alongside her and save the entire crew.

Not all life saving rescues are such a success. A few years later, in 1881, another violent storm struck the Norwegian barque *American*. She was sheltering in the calmer waters on the Welsh side of the Bristol Channel when the cable with which a tug was towing her to safety snapped. There was no choice but to transfer the crew to the tug and head for a safe harbour. But somehow the Norwegian crew forgot the ship's carpenter, who was below decks and unaware of his fate until he went up on deck to find himself abandoned and alone. The barque was blown across the Channel towards the Somerset coast. The carpenter managed to steer her to the less perilous shore at Blue Anchor and there waded up through the mud to the railway station where the startled station master, faced with someone covered from head to foot in mud and speaking in a foreign tongue, promptly put a gun to his head.

Captains Escott, Alfred Wedlake, J. Davis. A. Nicholas and Simon Nicholas

By 1899, Watchet had a new lifeboat, the *W. H. G. Kingston*. That November the trawler *Rosalie* sailed from Minehead in search of herring. The weather turned bad with little warning and soon a raging storm was blowing in the Bristol Channel. The *Rosalie* managed to return to Minehead but her crew of two were so exhausted they were unable to bring her in through the harbour entrance. Bitterly cold and weakened, they shouted as best they could to attract attention. Their cries were just heard above the roar of the sea and the Watchet lifeboat was launched. No sooner were they out into open water than the strength of the incoming tide and strong sou'westerly winds combined to take the lifeboat up the Channel towards Bridgwater Bay. It would be hours before the lifeboat would be able to get back to her home port, let alone further west along the coast to Minehead.

Meanwhile the plight of the two fishermen on board the *Rosalie* was worsening, their cries for help weakening as time passed. At the quayside, five local sea captains were deep in discussion. Could a smaller, lighter craft with a strong crew achieve success where the heavier lifeboat had failed? Captain Escott took command, to be joined by Alfred Wedlake, J. Davis and A. and S. Nicholas. Cheers erupted as they took to the oars and pulled towards the harbour mouth.

Just as they reached open water a huge wave hit the harbour wall and the men disappeared from view. The wave subsided and once again the gallant crew could be seen, still pulling towards the distressed fishermen. The small craft cut through the waves. One moment she was invisible, hidden behind the bank of a high wave, the next standing proud on the crest before plunging down into the next trough. Many a heart was in the mouth among the spectators ashore.

For some minutes, nothing could be seen at all and then the small rescue boat was spotted heading homeward for the harbour. The tension mounted as attempts were made to count those aboard. Cheers erupted as it was realised all the crew were safe and that the two fishermen were also on board.

Back at Watchet, the lifeboat and its crew finally returned after riding out the storm. Their reward was to be told that their lifeboat station was to be closed and a new one opened at Minehead. Such was their anger that a successful campaign was mounted to keep Watchet lifeboat station open, and it was only finally closed half a century later.

Burnham's Lifeboat

It's not just storms that take lives along the Somerset coast. Its mile after mile of mud flats have many a time entrapped an unwary visitor. A walk to Berrow Sands at low tide reveals the wreck of the S.S. *Nornen*, a Norwegian vessel which was wrecked in March 1897. Just the skeleton of her hull survives to provide a ghostly reminder of ships lost at sea. She was caught in a howling sou'westerly which swept her up the Bristol Channel. Conditions were appalling with driving snow and stinging sleet. Despite dropping anchor in Lundy Roads, the force of the wind and tide caused her anchors to drag and she drifted out of control towards the mud flats at Berrow. She was spotted at Burnham, her sails now torn to shreds, and the lifeboat was launched. The crew's battle to save their ship was already lost when the Burnham lifeboat came alongside, saving the lives of all on board, including the ship's dog.

A tragic day for the Rescue Services

Many visitors walk out to the remains of the *Nornen* when the tide is out. Unfortunately some venture beyond the wreck, unaware of the sinking sands ahead. In the summer of 2003, three young lads from County Tipperary were rescued from Steart Sands, just across the river from Burnham-on-Sea, by an RAF rescue helicopter. They had wandered a mile and a half out onto the mudflats, only to be trapped by the deceptive speed with which the incoming tide rushes in over the flats.

Not so lucky was young Lelaina Hall from Worcester. In June 2002, this five year old girl had wandered out onto the mudflats at Berrow and become trapped by the rising tide. The sands here are quite firm under foot until the tide invisibly creeps in underneath them. They then become quicksand. I watched from the shore as the rescue services tried to reach her. Her mother's partner had already tried to wade out to her and, despite his brave and desperate efforts, he also became trapped.

A lifeboat rescue was impossible, the tide was too far out. The rescue had to be launched from the shore or by air. Firemen using mud-sleds tried to get closer but the situation was impossible. Their feet just sank into the mud as they tried to move the sled forward. Suddenly Lelaina was no longer visible. Twenty minutes later a rescue helicopter arrived and spent the next half an hour searching for the young girl, but to no avail. Soon after, they spotted Lelaina's body, face down in the mud. I watched as her limp, lifeless form was winched into the helicopter where the crew began an attempt at resuscitation. She was later declared dead in Weston-super-Mare hospital.

I wish I hadn't been there. I wish I hadn't seen it. It's a scene that still haunts me. As the helicopter flew away, there on the shore stood her mother with members of the coastguard, the police, the fire brigade and an ambulance. Those men had done everything in their power to achieve a happier ending. The one thing they lacked which may have saved young Lelaina was a rescue Hovercraft. It struck me then that that scene would remain in my memory for many years to come, yet all those who serve in Somerset's emergency services face similar traumatic experiences day in and day out. Heroes one and all.

One positive outcome from the tragedy is that Burnham lifeboat station now has its long awaited rescue Hovercraft.

SIX

Rescues

The Timsbury Mining Disaster

'They're all heroes' was the response I had from one angry lady when I put the question, 'Are you aware of any particular heroes from the mines in North Somerset?' So hostile a reaction was in a way quite justified. I didn't tell her that my own grandfather had been killed in an horrific accident in a coal mine. It wasn't a moment for point scoring. Yet while I sympathise with her response, what I was after was one of those moments where an individual stands out from the crowd in performing a deed where the risk is measurably greater than the daily norm.

One such occasion came at Timsbury near Bath on a bitterly cold February day in 1895. The usual coal black, dust-covered surrounds of the pit head were carpeted in deep snow at the Conygre Collieries, just to the west of Timsbury. There were two entrances, one to the upper and one to the lower pit. Below ground these two areas were joined by a tunnel half a mile long. Almost a hundred and ninety men worked at the collieries, but fortunately at the time of the disaster few of them were underground. When coal production was in full swing, the pit-head bustled with activity. On the day concerned, it was fairly quiet. Two small teams totalling nine men entered the pit; two into the upper works and seven the lower. It was half past eight in the evening when the cages began their descent, taking the maintenance teams deep underground.

Two of the lower works team were due to enlarge the tunnel shaft which connected the upper and lower works. Although the shaft was high enough to allow coal-carrying trams to pass through, there was not enough head room for the pit ponies. Large chunks of the stone ceiling had to be blasted to create the extra height. A hole was drilled some three hundred yards into the shaft, the powder carefully placed, the fuse set and the men, both considerably experienced, withdrew. Moments later, the powder was fired and a devastating explosion took place, far greater than anticipated, killing the two men instantly. The cause of the explosion remains uncertain, but probably there was an unusual amount of coal dust in the atmosphere – which can ignite when the conditions are right.

Such was the force of the blast that trams were thrown into the air crashing into each other and the tunnel walls as they shattered. Massive rocks as big as cars were hurtled down the tunnels. The cage, in which those who entered the upper works had descended into the mine from the pit-head, was blasted back up its shaft until gravity regained control. Fortunately, although wrecked and useless, it became jammed before falling uncontrollably back down the shaft. The blast damage extended throughout the mine; one roof collapsed that was a thousand yards from the centre of the explosion.

At various points around the mine lay the bodies of five more men, their flesh scorched and charred. In like fashion, the pit ponies shared the same fate. Just two men escaped alive, George Fowler and John Fear. They had been examining a part of the mine which was served by a separate ventilation shaft and hence miraculously escaped.

Those who perished left four widows and numerous children. James Carter's wife was left with twelve children, ten of whom had not yet reached working age. For John Keeling's widow, it was one tragedy on top of another. Ten days earlier the inquest had been held into the death of her son, who had been fatally injured when his head collided with a bridge when travelling on top a railway carriage. George Harding, Joseph Bridges, John Gage, George Sperring and James Durham completed the role call of lost lives.

George Grice, Tom Short and Enoch Fricker

Above ground, those who had left the pit earlier heard the massive blast and could only stand in stunned silence, their coal-blackened faces in stark contrast against the white of the snow. A bitter wind blew up the hillside, adding its chill to the sombre mood of the miners. From amongst their number, three men stepped forward and volunteered to go down the shaft into the upper workings to see what could be done to rescue their fellow workers, who at this point it was hoped were alive. They had already realised that the pit-head machinery had been wrecked and any descent would have to be carried out using muscle power alone. A windlass was set up and one by one, George Grice, Tom Short and Enoch Fricker were lowered into the darkness. Such was the cold on that winter's day that at the surface the thermometer showed twenty nine degrees of frost. Working in such temperatures is almost impossible and as the men went deeper and deeper into the shaft, it dropped even further. Finally the three men had to admit defeat. They had to be winched back up to the surface before they lost all sense of feeling in their hands.

A second brave team made another attempt, this time reaching the working area. Initially they were able to progress along a horizontal shaft, scrambling over a fall of rock, but then were forced to retreat as the foul air rendered them semi-conscious and one miner had to be taken unconscious to the surface. Before going back, they met another rescue party who had entered the pit from the lower workings. By rigging up 'curtains' they were able to redirect the air flow and create a breathable environment in which to work. One by the one the bodies were found. On one charred body a watch ticked ominously. Once again foul air stopped their progress and they were forced to return to the surface.

By now it was twelve hours since the ill-fated maintenance team had made its descent. Despite the gallant efforts of the would be rescuers, the immediate attempt to rescue anyone alive was abandoned until the following day. It was realized that no one could have survived down below other than the two men who walked out alive. Late the following day, the bodies were all recovered and placed in a small outhouse near the entrance to the lower pit.

These were men who had lost their lives carrying out their daily work, each of them in their own way a hero just for facing the inherent risks that go with coal mining. But the real heroes were those who went down the mine in an attempt to rescue them. Following an explosion, the normal risks are multiplied a hundred fold, but still they put the lives of others before their own.

Herbert Golledge, Wellow

It was some five miles away from Timsbury that, on 26 February 1917, during the First World War, the bravery of a Wellow man earned him the Edward Vll medal. The weather conditions were similar to those at the time of the Timsbury disaster. A bitter wind blew across the Mendips. It was seven in the morning and the day shift was well under way at the Braysdown Colliery. George Weeks, the mine's under manager, was ready to return to the surface and had entered the cage at the bottom of the shaft leading up to the pit-head. Two cages operated in the same shaft, which also carried some cast iron water pipes.

Unbeknown to George, a rock or large piece of coal had fallen from the surface cage dislodging the fixings holding the pipes to the side of the shaft, leaving them dangling out into the cavity through which the cages would pass. As the surface cage began its descent, it collided with the projecting pipework, breaking it off. The lower cage was by now on its way to the pit-head. The falling pipe tore through its roof bringing the cage to a complete standstill and slamming into George Weeks, who was left semi-conscious with his head split open and a dislocated shoulder. The cage was wedged, making rescue from another cage impossible. It was dark and cold. The wind was blowing down the shaft, and George Weeks was lying on the floor of the cage bleeding profusely and in a state of severe shock.

Some 240 feet overhead, Herbert Golledge was working in a side gallery which branched off from the vertical shaft used by the cages. He was a quiet married man who was employed as a hitcher, someone who unhitches the trams and puts them into the cages to be taken to the surface. He was somewhat on the reserved side, but nonetheless a strong enough character. He heard the crash and knew instinctively that a fellow miner was in trouble. But reaching the wedged cage wouldn't be easy. The shaft was lined with small wooden projections which could be used as footholds. Disregarding the risk to himself, Herbert Golledge began the treacherous descent of the shaft, climbing cautiously down the ice-covered projections. A dim flickering light was provided by his miner's lamp, which he hung from his belt to leave his hands free. He could hear Weeks groaning as he neared the cage.

Reaching its roof, he climbed inside to where Weeks was still bleeding heavily and slipping in and out of consciousness. The temperature was well below zero. Weeks was losing blood fast. Herbert Golledge took off his coat and shirt, using the latter as a tourniquet to stem the flow of blood from the wound in Weeks' head. His coat he wrapped round the injured miner to help maintain his body temperature.

And that is how the next four hours were spent. Golledge was freezing cold as, stripped to the waist, he tended his patient. He could hear the rescue work going on above him as his fellow miners on the surface struggled to get the cages moving once more. Finally Golledge felt the cage lumber cautiously back into life before gradually ascending to the surface. After immediate treatment at the pit-head, George Weeks was taken home, where the following weeks were spent in bed slowly recovering from his injuries.

A week later, members of the mining community gathered at the Shoscombe School hall where Herbert Golledge was presented with a cheque for six guineas and a gold watch engraved to commemorate his courage. In making the presentation, Mr. Gregory, the mine manager, referred to those fighting in the trenches in Europe, noting that members of some communities regarded the miners as cowards for not serving in the armed forces. And yet here was an example of bravery equal of any on the Western Front. George Weeks, still suffering from his injuries, had been brought to the hall and spoke warmly of Herbert's heroism, raising the cheers of all present as he shook him by the hand. Further recognition was to come when Golledge received £10 from the Carnegie Hero Fund.

It was some weeks later on a Friday evening, when Herbert Golledge left his home at Railway Lane in Wellow to travel up to London, his first trip to the capital. The following morning he entered Buckingham Palace, and His Majesty King George V presented him with the Edward Vll medal for gallantry, shaking him warmly by the hand. On one side of the medal was the profile of Edward Vll, on the other a depiction of a miner attending an injured comrade, above which is simply the word 'Courage'.

Beating the Blizzards

Frank Vigars and Douglas Batchelor

Somerset is, generally speaking, blessed with mild winters, but once in a while it is subject to one of those classic cold winters which are talked about for generations to come. The remote communities on the high ground of Exmoor suffer more than most on such occasions. One such winter was that of 1940 when freezing conditions gripped the whole of war-torn Europe. During January heavy snows fell on Exmoor leaving drifts of six to eight feet deep. At Withypool, 42 degrees of frost were recorded and from 27 January to 3 February, freezing rain fell almost continuously. It was the harshest winter since 1890.

Fifty-six-year-old Frank Vigars was a mason on the Fortescue Estate and with his wife helped run the sub post office at Simonsbath, Somerset's most westerly village and set in a remote valley in the heart of Exmoor. Frank Vigars was a tough and determined character who took his responsibilities seriously. When the postal van was unable to get through from South Molton, he delivered the mail come what may, crawling through the snow, on hands and knees at times, to ensure the post got through. Hedgerows and farm gates were totally blanketed by snow, allowing Frank to walk over the top of them and in a straighter line than was usual. His daily round trip to Exford of seven miles took almost as many hours to complete, but Frank maintained the tradition of the daily delivery throughout the winter.

In Exford itself, forty-year-old Douglas Batchelor kept a general grocery store where he lived with his wife Rosemary and their three children. Ensuring the local community was properly provisioned was his clear duty, not just in Exford, but neighbouring Simonsbath and its outlying communities and farms. He organised supply parties to get the provisions through, who between them filled sacks with bread, tinned food and other essentials before setting out over the moor and battling through snowdrifts as much as eight feet high. Local knowledge and familiarity with the shape of the land were crucial, as most normal landmarks were buried beneath the snow.

Delivery services such as these may seem a bit dramatic for those living in the relative comfort of suburbia, but were critical for Exmoor's remote communities. Exmoor winters can be unforgiving. Next to Exford's churchyard gate is a memorial to twenty-four-year-old Amos Cann, caught in a blizzard in 1891 while walking home from Porlock and not found for three weeks.

PC Trott and Special Constable Frank Mullins

1947 saw Arctic conditions return with a vengeance. For six consecutive weeks the temperature remained below zero. From January, to March, a succession of severe blizzards struck the county. The March blizzard was especially cruel, lasting an unrelenting thirty six hours.

As early as January the temperature was 20 degrees below and the villages of Exford and Simonsbath were once again cut off. Post war food rationing meant that there were no surpluses and what little was on the shelves had to be rationed still further. Attempts by the local authority to clear the road between the two villages had ended in failure. The snow was so hard-packed it even broke the snow plough. Once again the daily treks on foot were instigated to get supplies through. It was to be three months before any vehicles reached Simonsbath.

Just before the January blizzard, two members of the RAF had been sent to guard a plane that had crashed at Larkbarrow. They took with them tinned rations and a coal brazier, but no one anticipated the severity of the blizzard which struck whilst they were guarding the plane. The fine powdery snow was blown inside the bonnet of their lorry, causing the engine to freeze. Their food and water froze solid, and they lost their meagre supply of coal beneath a drift. After two days they were close to death from exposure and hypothermia – but help was on its way. The RAF station at which the two men were based had notified the local police of their plight and asked them to organise a rescue.

PC Trott and Special Constable Frank Mullins set out on horseback across the moor. Inevitably, conditions worsened and they were forced to leave the horses at a moorland farm. The next three miles on foot turned into six as the two policemen floundered their way around eight foot drifts. They found the airmen about a mile from the plane, huddled together in their truck and at the point of total despair after two days without food or drink.

The Winter of 1962/1963

If anything, the winter of 1963 was even worse for the outlying parts of Somerset. The snow fell between Christmas and the New Year. On Exmoor drifts of up to ten feet were common, and some were as deep as thirty feet. Snow still lingered as late as Easter. But by 1963, communications, other than by road, were much improved and it was the helicopter crews who were the heroes, flying in food for the villagers, bales of hay for sheep, medicines and doctors for the sick and injured.

In addition, the villages organised their own communication and delivery systems. Men from neighbouring villages would set out at more or less the same time, walking towards each other. Loaves of bread, other food and the mail would be passed this way from one village to the next until they reached their destination. Teams of vehicles went out in convoys, each taking winching equipment to help them through the drifts so as to reach the provisions so important to the survival of the isolated farmsteads on places like Exmoor, the Quantocks and Mendips.

It's occasions such as these, when whole communities pull together, that individual acts of courage take second place to the ways in which a crisis or disaster can unite and strengthen even the most fearful. Extraordinary times can make heroes out of the most ordinary people.

Water borne rescues

Somerset is a coastal county. Much of the 200 square miles that comprise the Somerset Levels lie only a little above sea level. The Bristol Channel has the second highest tidal range in the world; a tide of 44 feet has been recorded at Bridgwater. Couple this with hundreds of miles of rivers and drains, and the potential for inland flooding is all too obvious. Even on higher ground, flash floods can create havoc and cause considerable loss of life. Heavy rainfall on the hills and high moors of Somerset can result in levels rising almost without warning as the swifter-flowing streams drain into the slower-moving rivers on the Levels.

George Wines, Edward Blake and John Jones

In mid-November 1894, Somerset endured three days and nights of continuous rain. The River Parrett burst in banks in many places, including at Langport where Bow Street was soon under five feet of water. To the north, Frome and Wells were inundated with water rushing down from the Mendips. Many of the villages in South Somerset were cut off by the floods. Early winter flooding is a frequent occurrence and the locals have learned to cope with its problems. So perhaps it was with some complacency that James Martin set off from Yeovil with his horse and cart to complete his delivery round of groceries, drapery and gloves to the villages around South Petherton.

As he approached Shores Bridge, just east of South Petherton where the A303 now crosses the River Parrett, with a passenger on board as well as his groceries, the water deepened. Suddenly the current swept the cart, its horse and passengers sideways. The horse lost its footing and, as it keeled over to one side, the cart tipped and the entire party were whipped away by the flood water. Crashing into a bank and then a tree, the cart came to a temporary halt, avoiding certain death for the two men in the turbulent main flow of the river. The horse drowned, unable to keep its head above the water. Martin and his passenger clung to the upturned cart and shouted for help. Swimming to safety was out of the question, such was the force of the water.

Fortunately their cries were heard and George Wines came to the rescue. He worked at Bridge House for Edward Blake, who employed around thirty men on his farm. Realising the seriousness of the situation, George summoned his employer and fellow worker John Jones and they went to the rescue. An initial attempt to reach the victims by horse and cart failed. The only way the marooned men could be reached was if someone waded out far enough to reach them by throwing a rope. It was Blake who did so, at great risk of being swept away. Eventually he was close enough to reach them with one good throw. Cold and exhausted, the two men were pulled to safety.

Thomas Griffiths

In 1859, the Royal Humane Society presented a medal to Thomas Griffiths, a Bridgwater pilot, for rescuing Thomas Warren from drowning. This in itself is perhaps not particularly outstanding but what makes Thomas Griffiths stand out from the crowd is that Thomas Warren was the fifteenth person he had saved, and probably was not the last. Drowning in the River Parrett or docks was a regular occurrence at Bridgwater, specially during its mid-nineteenth century heyday as a port.

Joseph Seaman

Joseph Seaman was another Bridgwater man who made a habit of rescues. The *Bridgwater Mercury* of July 29th 1896 reported the episode. '*On Friday afternoon a little girl between three and four years old named Beatrice Louisa Browning, whose parents live in King Street, accidentally fell off the quay wall opposite the Punch Bowl a considerable height, into the river. A man named Joseph Seaman living at 124 Bristol Road, hurriedly climbed down a chain and dropping upon the mud, seized the child and rescued it. Beyond a severe shaking and the fright occasioned, the girl had not, happily, sustained any injury, and was at once conveyed to her home.*'

But this was only one of many river rescues carried out Joseph Seaman. It appears Seaman also started something of a family tradition, for he had a son of the same name who was also responsible for the rescue of a young child, with considerable help from the family Airedale.

Kenneth Meadowcroft and Dennis Brown

As a lad, I grew up near the site of the old fire station in the Cattle Market at Bath Road in Bridgwater. Whilst Wednesday was market day, bringing with it all the activities of a bustling market town, the rest of the week had plenty to offer by way of diversion, and the cattle pens and disused clay pits at the back of the fire station provided ample entertainment for a young boy.

It was there on 25 May 1963, that three year old Paul Wiltshire of Union Street was playing with his older brother. Then tragedy struck. Young Paul slipped and fell into the deep and murky waters of one of the pits. As his brother stood on the bank, Paul sank invisibly to the bottom. Unable to see Paul, his older brother ran as fast as his legs would carry him to the nearby fire station. There he raised the alarm and, without further ado, Firemen Kenneth Meadowcroft and Dennis Brown together with Leading Fireman Ken Phillips rushed to the scene.

Almost without hesitation, Ken Meadowcroft kicked off his boots and jumped into the pit, landing in mud up to his waist. A quick search of his muddy surroundings revealed no sign of the three-year-old. Fixing a line to himself, he dived into deeper water. Every second was vital. Indeed the lad might already be dead. If he had been under water throughout the time it took his brother to raise the alarm and the firemen to return, it would surely be too late.

Groping around the bottom, Ken was unable to find the youngster. Surfacing for breath, he dived once more. Still no success, and the minutes were ticking by. Three more attempts, diving down to the shelving bottom as he moved further from the bank. Ken's perseverance owed much to his training, but also to the thought of his two children safely at home.

On the sixth attempt, he found Paul's body, lifeless and limp, face down in the mud at the bottom of the pit. A good eight minutes must have passed from the moment Paul fell into the pit to the time Ken brought the pitiful little body to the surface. Initially, there were no signs of life as the exhausted Ken passed the lad over to Dennis Brown, who at once applied mouth to mouth resuscitation. In a few minutes young Paul was breathing again. He was rushed off to hospital in a critical condition but managed to pull through, thanks to the efforts and knowledge of Dennis Brown and Kenneth Meadowcroft, who himself required hospital treatment after the ordeal.

Paul Stubbles and Paul Williams, Firefighters

On August 6th 1997, following three days of heavy rain, the White Watch members of Taunton Fire Brigade were pumping water from the flooded cellar of the Cross Keys public house at Norton FitzWarren. The nearby tributary of the River Tone had risen to such a level that it had burst its banks.

Suddenly the alarm was raised. A woman had fallen into the river and had been swept down to a bridge, where she was hanging on to the side of the parapet desperately trying to avoid being swept under the small gap now left at the top of the bridge arch. Imagine hanging on by your fingers to the frame of a open doorway with a flood rushing through. The fire crew pumping out the cellar raced to the nearby bridge. There they saw the head and arms of the woman, who was just keeping herself above the flood water. Firefighter Paul

Stubbles was tied to a rope and lowered over the parapet into the water, being held in place by another firefighter, Bob Storey. He immediately grabbed her by one wrist to ensure she was not swept away. With her other hand she still clung to the bridge.

Fellow firefighter Paul Williams was tied to another rescue line. On the end of his line were Colin Clarke, Colin Everley and Darren Mockridge, all of whom were on the bank and positioned so as to be able to haul him to safety should he be dragged under by the force of the current. It would clearly be easier to pull the lady to the bank than attempt to lift her up over the parapet of the bridge. As Paul Williams entered the river, he was swept away by the current. A second attempt was made and this time he got much closer to the woman. He was almost near enough to reach her when his worst fears were realised. She lost her grip. Paul Stubbles, suspended from the bridge, was now in danger of losing his hold on her and was equally at risk himself of being swept under the bridge. Only one firefighter, Bob Storey, was taking the strain on the other end of the line. If Paul Stubbles was to be hauled to safety he would have to let go of the lady whose life now depended on him.

Those on the bank could see the desperate nature of the situation. Another member of the crew entered the river, unsecured and with no rescue line attached. He got close enough to take the lady's other arm, but immediately began to sink beneath the surface, forced down by the power of the rushing water. In order to save himself, he managed to grab the line to which Paul Williams was tied and which ran back to the river bank. By now the lady had been dragged beneath the surface and was in danger of drowning. Despite the risk, Paul Stubbles maintained his grip on her wrist and managed to lift her back up to the surface. Meanwhile, Paul Williams and the other officer, who now shared his line, were hauled back to the river bank.

Paul Stubbles remained in the river, struggling to keep himself and the lady afloat. Realising how desperate the situation had become, Paul Williams re-entered the water from higher upstream. In this way he hoped to swim far enough out into the river to be swept down with the flood and re-establish contact with the lady. This time the attempt was successful. He grabbed the lady around the waist. At long last, Paul Stubbles was able to release his grip. As he did so, Paul Williams and the lady were immediately dragged under water by the force of the current. But the rescue line held and slowly they were pulled as a pair towards the river bank and safety. The lady was later taken to hospital where she recovered. Back on the bridge, Paul Stubbles, exhausted, was hauled back onto dry land.

What had started as a routine call-out to pump out flooded premises had turned into a major drama. It was a situation where the importance of a well-trained team was crucial, where men exposed to danger could safely put their faith in the professionalism of their colleagues. The rescue would not have been successful without the efforts of the entire team but it was the bravery of Firefighters Paul Stubbles and Paul Williams which was singled out. Their actions were later recognised by the award of the Queen's Commendation for Bravery.

The Floods of 1952

Those who remember the 1950's will remember the disastrous flooding of the Devon town of Lynmouth, when the normally peaceful River Lyn became a raging torrent, destroying bridges and sweeping away homes. But that was over the border in Devon. On the Somerset side of Exmoor, other disasters were unfolding.

Stan Curtis, Denzil Curtis and Bob Barrow

Stan Curtis with his brother Denzil and brother-in-law, Bob Barrow, were returning home on their motor-bikes and had difficulty getting through the flooded roads. Reaching the Exmoor Forest Hotel in Simonsbath, the group realised something was amiss. All the lights were off in the hotel. Stopping to look, they heard the voice of Mr. Holman, the owner, calling desperately for help. Water had been pouring down from Ashcombe Bottom, had entered the hotel at the back and could find no way out. Gradually the hotel was filling with water. It was already half way up the dining room windows and still rising. It was mid August and the hotel was full of guests who had retreated to the temporary safety of the upstairs level. The water level was soon past the tops of the windows and there was a real danger of the building collapsing with everyone inside.

Stan quickly realised that they needed to break the windows or doors if there was to be any chance of the waters subsiding. As fast as they could, they broke as many windows as possible – but it was still not enough. They would have to break down the front door. They knew that in doing so they were liable to be swept away by the force of the escaping water. Their only hope was that a gate further down the path from the front door would provide a temporary safety net. They closed the gate and turned their attention to the door. The plan worked. As the door gave way, the water gushed through, sweeping them straight down the path and into the gate, which they clung onto until the water lost its power.

The hotel was an old building and it is safe to assume that, without the quick thinking of the three men, the front wall of the hotel would have collapsed with considerable loss of life. Cold, wet and exhausted, the three men made their way up the path and into the hotel as the waters subsided. Once at the bar they granted themselves a bottle of rum, which they finished off between them. Later the clean up process started. Tractors pulled the sodden carpets out through the broken windows and tons of gravel were cleared from inside the hotel. Apart from the rum, Stan's only reward for his part in saving lives was an insurance payout of 3s 6d to have his suit cleaned!

Eric James

A story with a tragic ending, but one which includes the ultimate test of human bravery is that of Eric James. It was 1901 and there were just three days to go to Christmas. It was a period of celebration and anticipation, in which the ice-covered ponds around Chard provided additional excitement. One day, Sarah Melhuish took her young son and Eric James, the son of a neighbour, to enjoy the ice on the frozen reservoir outside the town. For some years the reservoir had been a popular winter spot for ice skating and a number of skaters were already on the ice when Sarah arrived.

Sarah was distracted by the sight of a motor car which had stopped on a nearby bridge, an unusual sight in 1901. Tragically, during that momentary distraction, young Eric had ventured onto the ice and fallen though. Rising to the occasion, fifteen-year-old Lawrence Hussey, another neighbour from the same street, crawled onto the ice in an attempt to rescue Eric, who was now struggling in the freezing waters. As Lawrence approached Eric, he lay flat on the ice to spread his weight, hoping it would not break beneath him. He reached down into the water and slowly began to pull Eric onto the ice.

Disaster then struck a second time. Lawrence felt the ice beneath him crack. The combined weight of the two boys caused the already weakened ice to break away and Lawrence slid head first into the ice cold waters. A nearby Great Western Railway fireman, Alfred Pearce, had seen what was happening. Lying face down and flat on the ice, he began to inch forward. All around him he could hear the ice cracking. As he closed in on the two boys, he could see Lawrence visibly weakening in the struggle to keep himself and young Eric afloat. The chill of the water was taking its toll. His energy was waning and he could fight no further to save himself and the young lad.

Alfred could only watch as, just out of reach, he saw the two lads slowly slip under the surface. Alfred managed to get back to the bank just as the remainder of the ice broke. Later that evening, a specially constructed raft was launched and the two bodies were recovered. Lawrence Hussey's heroism in trying to save young Eric James, and in sacrificing his own life in the process, was recognised by the townsfolk of Chard who erected a drinking trough in his memory. It survives today at Millfield.

Have a Go Heroes

How often do we read an account of some act of heroism that ends with someone saying, 'I just did what anyone would have done?' And yet we know that all too often it is easier not to get involved, to simply stand back or pass by.

Andrew Reeves, Ruth Reeves, James Reeves, and David Davies

One classic example of the Good Samaritan who didn't pass by was Andrew Reeves, a builder from Hutton who, in the summer of 2003, was driving home at the end of a day's work from the village of Woolavington. With him were his wife, Ruth, and twenty one year old son, James. Leaving the M5 motorway at the Burnham-on-Sea junction, he noticed a car which had just left the road and overturned into a ditch. Without thinking, Andrew pulled in and ran over to the car. There was the smell of burning and the car was already on fire. Bravely, and at great risk to himself, he climbed over the bonnet until he could see the elderly driver inside the car. Although the man didn't

Herbert Pitman MBE (1877-1961) – seen below on the left with 2nd Officer Charles Lightoller on his right – was 3rd Officer on the *Titanic* when the doomed liner struck an iceberg on its maiden voyage to New York in April 1912. Pitman was born at Sutton Montis near Castle Cary, finally retiring from a life afloat to the small village of Pitcombe, where a black marble headstone marks his grave.

Minehead's first motorised lifeboat being launched in the 1930s. The lifeboats stationed along Somerset's coast have been involved in many rescues since the county's first station was opened at Watchet in 1874.

Lower Conygre Pit, Timsbury, the scene of a mining disaster in 1895 which left seven miners dead.

This photograph of a car amongst the snowdrifts on Exmoor gives some idea of the ferocity of the blizzards in the winter of 1947, when many of the small farming communities on Exmoor were effectively cut off for several months.

Bridgwater quayside in the 1890s, where Thomas Griffiths and Joseph Seaman saved many from drowning.

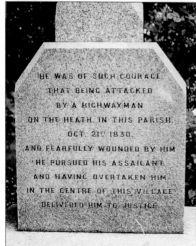

HE WAS OF SUCH COURAGE
THAT BEING ATTACKED
BY A HIGHWAYMAN
ON THE HEATH IN THIS PARISH
OCT. 21ˢᵗ 1830,
AND FEARFULLY WOUNDED BY HIM
HE PURSUED HIS ASSAILANT
AND HAVING OVERTAKEN HIM
IN THE CENTRE OF THIS VILLAGE
DELIVERED HIM TO JUSTICE

ABOVE Firefighters Paul Stubbles and Paul Williams of Taunton Fire Brigade, together with their wives, at the presentation of their award of the Queen's Commendation for Bravery in 1997 after rescuing a woman from the flooded River Tone.

LEFT The memorial to Charles Hardwick in Congresbury churchyard. Hardwick was attacked by a highwayman in 1830, 'and fearfully wounded by him, he pursued his assailant and having overtaken him in the centre of this village, delivered him to justice.'

A girl photographed in about 1900 wearing a pair of artificial legs made by James Gillingham (1839-1924), a Chard boot and shoemaker.

John Stringfellow (1799-1883) of Chard, and now regarded as one of the inventors of the aeroplane.

The monoplane built by John Stringfellow and which completed a ten yard powered flight inside a Chard lace mill in 1848.

The first Christmas card was sent out by Sir Henry Cole in 1843 so as to avoid having to write lots of individual letters to his friends and family.

Sir George Williams (1821-1905) who was born in Dulverton and went on to found the YMCA, which today has over thirty million members.

Mary Rand MBE, making her world record long jump of 22 feet 2¼ inches at the Olympic Games in Tokyo in 1964. As well as winning the gold medal for the long jump, she also won a silver medal in the pentathlon and a bronze medal in the sprint relay. Mary Rand's jump is recorded in slabs of limestone set into the pavement in Wells market square, the city where she was born.

The high altitude balloonists Andy Elson and Colin Prescott meet the Queen. Andy Elson lives in Masbury near Wells. For his record-breaking eighteen day flight from Spain to Japan in 1999 he was awarded the prestigous Royal Aero Club's Gold Medal, whose previous recipients include many of the great pioneers of manned flight, from the Wright brothers to Neil Armstrong.

move, Andrew realised that he might well be still alive.

He bent over and pulled at the door handle, which refused to budge. He kicked desperately at the windscreen but the toughened laminate would not yield. Ruth and James watched in horror, terrified that at any second the car could explode with the loss of two lives. Andrew called to his wife to fetch a hammer from his van. Frantically she searched and found a lump hammer. As she hurried back to the scene of the accident, she could see flames licking round the seat of Andrew's trousers.

'Andrew, you're on fire!' Ruth shouted. By this time another motorist, David Davies from Burnham-on-Sea, had arrived to help. Andrew smashed the side window. The driver was now showing some signs of consciousness but was strapped in and Andrew was unable to reach the belt buckle. The flames grew ever higher. The fellow motorist produced a Stanley knife and they cut the driver's belt. Standing on the side of the car, Andrew Reeves, who had been joined by his son James, managed to haul the man out. As they dragged him away, the car turned into a sheet of flames. Moments later it exploded, each exploding tyre creating its own shock wave and reminding those looking on that the danger was not yet over.

Ruth stood at the side of the road, shaking. Her adrenalin rush subsided, allowing her time to reflect on what might have been. Within minutes the car was a blackened, burnt out wreck. What if Andrew had just passed by like so many other drivers? What if he hadn't the courage to stand on the bonnet of a burning car or lacked the initiative to remember the hammer in his van? His reactions had been almost instantaneous. Throughout the rescue, the Reeves' family and David Davies had shown selfless compassion for the trapped driver and bravery of the highest order. Later Andrew commented to Kelly Crane, a reporter from the *Weston Mercury*, 'I didn't think about my life at the time. Looking back I suppose I was in danger but at the time instincts kick in and adrenaline takes over.' The driver of the vehicle later left hospital with only minor injuries thanks to the courage of his rescuers.

In December 2003, it was announced by the Avon and Somerset Constabulary that Andrew, Ruth and James Reeves along with David Davies were all to receive a Society for the Protection of Life from Fire award.

Charles Capell Hardwick

The story of a Somerset farmer who happened to be in the wrong place at the wrong time is commemorated on a memorial stone in the churchyard at Congresbury, which reads, *'He was of such courage that being attacked by a highwayman on the heath in this parish October 21st 1830, and fearfully wounded by him, he pursued his assailant and having overtaken him in the centre of this village, delivered him to justice'*.

The inscription tells us little, but the story is one of tremendous courage and fortitude. Thirty-one-year-old Charles Hardwick had been to Bristol market, and he was on his way home with a considerable sum of money in his purse. He had only travelled a few miles when he was joined by Richard Hewlett, a distant relative. They rode together, Charles enjoying the company and conversation, no doubt feeling safer in the company of another. He was within a mile of his farm when his companion unexpectedly swung his horse around and fired a pistol at him, the bullet penetrating deep into his shoulder. Hewlett soon realised he had not killed his target and quickly galloped off. Despite his wound, Charles Hardwick gave chase. His only weapon was his riding crop, surely no match for a pistol.

Gaining ground, he galloped alongside Hewlett, grabbing his quarry as he did so. He was beginning to overpower his assailant when Hewlett suddenly pulled out a hidden dagger and stabbed Hardwick, the blade penetrating right up to the hilt and narrowly missing his lungs.

The struggle continued until Hardwick, no doubt considerably weakened, was thrown off his horse. It was Hewlett's best chance to escape. He galloped off again, leaving the injured man on the ground. But Hardwick wasn't finished. Now with two severe injuries, he climbed back into the saddle and continued the chase. He was closing in when Hewlett almost galloped straight into a coach coming the other way and which appeared unexpectedly around a bend. Horse and rider crashed to the ground. Hardwick and his horse were now so close that they piled in on top of them. The occupants of the coach assumed they were witnessing a drunken brawl and hurried on, but before long some villagers arrived and Hewlett was arrested.

Over the weeks which followed, Hardwick's condition slowly

improved. Indeed, so critical were his wounds that the police took statements from him on the assumption he would die before telling the full story. Hewlett was found guilty of attempted murder and executed. Hardwick died aged fifty, after which the commemorative memorial in Congresbury was erected as a permanent reminder of his bravery.

SEVEN

For the Greater Good

There are those who have never had to face a life or death situation demanding the highest level of courage, yet in their own way have contributed to the common good.

James Gillingham

Sometimes an inventor comes along who is less interested in the prospect of commercial success than by what he might be able to achieve for his fellow man. Such a person was James Gillingham of Chard. James Gillingham was born in 1839 and became Chard's most fashionable boot and shoe maker. The turning point in his career was due to an accident in 1863 in which another Chard man lost his arm whilst firing a cannon to celebrate the Silver Jubilee of Queen Victoria's coronation. So moved was James Gillingham by the poor man's dilemma that he produced an artificial limb for him made from wood and leather. The medical profession was astounded by the success of the newly fitted arm, so much so that he abandoned shoe making in favour of making false arms and legs. By 1903, the firm of James Gillingham & Sons had provided over 7,000 disabled men and women with false limbs, enabling many to lead virtually normal lives. Between 1914 and 1918 the Chard premises of Monmouth House became a centre for casualties returning from the Western Front and the establishment was recognised as a centre of excellence in its field.

James Gillingham died in 1924 leaving behind his legacy to the world of prosthetics, and the firm he founded produced artificial limbs right through until the 1960s.

John Stringfellow

Another man who lived in Chard, and whose legacy lives on today in ways he could never have imagined, is John Stringfellow. He was born in 1799 in Sheffield, moving with his family to Nottingham as a teenager. Nottingham owed its prosperity to lace and in 1815 the young Stringfellow was apprenticed to a bobbin and carriage maker. Four years later he was sent to Chard to install machines in Mill Lane. Before long he set up his own business as a bobbin and carriage manufacturer and over the years developed a considerable reputation for quality products. He also developed and manufactured steam engines. In parallel with this activity, William Henson, a Chard lace making industrialist, in 1842 had taken out a patent for an aeroplane. A model was built and demonstrated in London. It was a complete disaster.

So Henson returned to Chard and began a working partnership with John Stringfellow. Their attempts to construct a prototype aeroplane proved fruitless. Henson lost interest, moved to London and married, later emigrating to America where he patented a safety razor.

Undeterred, Stringfellow continued on alone developing variations of the original design with a 20 foot wingspan. In 1847, when the prototype was finished, a team of workmen carried it up onto Bala Down under cover of darkness for a test flight. The secrecy reflected his sense of humiliation at the mockery he was subject to from local folk who failed to take his ideas seriously. Unfortunately, the weight of the dew on the silk covering the frame proved an insurmountable obstacle, and his plane stayed firmly on the ground. For nearly two months he continued his attempts but all were unsuccessful.

Undeterred, he began again from scratch. He abandoned the ideas he had been working on with Henson and developed new designs of his own. With a 10 foot wingspan, timber spars and silk fabric skin, the new plane was powered by a small steam engine fitted into a gondola slung beneath the fuselage. With two propellers, rotating in opposite directions for stability, his design lacked any form of vertical fin to help guide it in a specific direction. The least wind disturbance would have affected the direction of its flight, and so the maiden flight took place inside one of Chard's lace mills, where air movement was negligible. Although this improved Stringfellow's ability to control the plane's direction, it brought with it its own problems. The wingspan of the aeroplane, weighing about 8 pounds, was 10 feet and the width of the building was just 17, hence a leeway on either side of just over 3 feet. To allow for this, the aircraft was guided along a fixed wire for the first 10 yards. The room itself was only 22 yards in length and hence a maximum unassisted flight was never going to exceed ten yards. The first attempt was something of a failure. Once the plane left the wire, it pointed upwards, the engine cut out and it fell swiftly back to the ground on its tail. But lessons were learned from this failed attempt and, in 1848, Stringfellow triumphantly completed an unguided flight of ten yards before breaking through a canvas screen erected to prevent it flying into the end wall of the building.

His work continued with his son Frederick. However, it appears that having conquered powered flight, he then lost interest in it, perhaps unable to see beyond his initial achievement. In 1866 the Aeronautical Society of Great Britain was formed, renewing Stringfellow's interest. He and Frederick abandoned the monoplane in favour of a triplane, developing a one horse power steam engine weighing just 40 pounds to power it. In 1868 their triplane, the most famous of their machines, was exhibited at the Crystal Palace in London. These were the world's first examples of powered flight. The triplane could only make a descending glide and could not sustain itself in level flight. However, it provided the design which was to influence the successful biplanes and triplanes to follow.

A bronze model of the 1848 plane now stands in Chard's Fore Street. The nearby museum has an excellent exhibition describing his achievement and a plaque marks his house in the High Street. He died in 1883 and his grave in the local cemetery is also marked with a plaque.

Henry Cole – gave us the Christmas Card

Have you ever wondered who invented the first Christmas card? The credit belongs to Sir Henry Cole, who was born in Bath in 1808 and was the son of a guardsman. In later life he became a founding director of the South Kensington Museum, later to be renamed the Victoria and Albert Museum. He was also closely associated with the Great

Exhibition of 1851, was involved with the inception of the postal system and the construction of the Albert Hall. He wrote books and journals and served as an assistant to the Public Records Office, which he helped to organise. These various roles may appear to have little to do with Christmas, but they reflect an exceedingly busy life and one which left little time for paperwork at home.

At Christmas it was then common practice to write letters expressing best wishes to friends, family and both old and new acquaintances. But Sir Henry found it impossible to get his written in the time available. And so he asked an artist friend, John Calcott Horsley, to produce an illustrated card with a simple seasonal message which could be reproduced and sent to all his friends.

The first edition of these cards was printed on stiff folded card and portrayed a simple family scene, with those depicted raising a glass of red wine as a toast to the recipient. The card carried the message 'A Merry Christmas and a Happy New Year to You'. It was 1843 and the first Christmas card had been born – though not without a little scandal. The portrait included a lady holding a glass of wine from which a young girl was taking a sip. Some members of society were shocked by this apparent condoning of under age drinking. It was coincidentally the same year that Charles Dickens published *A Christmas Carol*.

Sufficient copies of that original card were produced for almost a thousand to go on sale to the public at a shilling each. Only a dozen survive today. In 2001, one of them was auctioned for £22,500. It did include Sir Henry's signature and was addressed to his 'Granny and Auntie Char', but even a lesser example would still be expected to fetch about £5,000.

Within three years of that first card, the practice of sending Christmas cards had been established, especially amongst the upper classes. By 1870 the introduction of the half penny post had reduced the costs to an affordable level. A wider audience adopted the greeting card practice, which soon became so popular that the postal service struggled to keep up with the increased demand. By 1900 an extra 12 million letters and cards were being delivered during Christmas week. Today almost every High Street can boast a greeting cards shop, such has been the impact of Henry Coles' idea, and almost 2 billion cards are sold each year in the United Kingdom alone.

George Williams – founder of the YMCA

The YMCA is one of the largest youth organisations in the world and was founded in poverty stricken inner London. But it was the contrast between that squalor and the rural background of a Somerset lad's youth, combined with a strong Christian conviction, which provided the inspiration for its foundation.

George Williams was born at Ashway Farm, Dulverton, in October 1821, the son of Amos and Elisabeth Williams, a farming family. It appears he may have been a somewhat reckless child, angering his father by overturning a hay cart. He left home at the age of fourteen and travelled to Bridgwater, where he was apprenticed in 1836 to Henry William Holmes, the town's leading draper with thirty employees. He later described how, 'I entered Bridgwater a careless, thoughtless, godless, swearing young fellow.'

He left the town a devout Christian, following his joining the congregation at the Zion Chapel in Friarn Street in 1837. He later said, 'I first learned in Bridgwater to love my dear Lord and Saviour for what he had done for me . . . I was on the downward road . . . They told me in this town of Bridgwater how to escape. Confess your sins, accept Christ, trust in Him, yield your heart to the Saviour.' George Williams declared that he was prepared to do just that and from then on his motto was, 'It is not how little but how much we can do for others.' By 1839 he had pledged abstinence and was on the chapel committee.

It was while in Bridgwater that he first developed the idea of a young man's Christian association. He recognised that the need for the association was greatest in London and that, if he were to make a success of it, London was where he was most likely to raise the necessary funding. In 1841, he left Somerset and moved to the capital. He was immediately struck by the appalling working conditions. Life as a draper's assistant was close to slavery. Sixteen hour days were commonplace. Most of the 150,000 young men and women employed in the drapery industry were under twenty years old and lived in crude accommodation provide by their employers. George found solace in the company of fellow workers. He was soon holding prayer meetings in his lodgings and bible study sessions with other young drapery employees who had similar convictions to his own.

In June 1844, he arranged for a number of like thinking men to meet in his bedroom, where on the wall hung the slogan 'God First'. The twelve men agreed to create the Young Men's Christian Association. They thought carefully about the title, deliberately avoiding calling it the Young Christian Men's Association as they wanted to include even those who were not practising Christians. Initially their aims were to include only the employees of other drapery houses. This they did by hiring halls and providing lectures and entertainment. Many influential people threw their weight behind the movement and its early growth was rapid.

In parallel with his development of the YMCA, George prospered as a tradesman, eventually running his own business. In all his dealings, he endeavoured to be fair and honest, not just with suppliers and customers but equally with his employees. He was instrumental in introducing an early closing day for the benefit of his staff, a practice which was widely imitated throughout the drapery trade. He also set aside two thirds of his profits to help fund his charitable works.

In 1851, YMCA groups were set up in Montreal and Boston. In 1855 the YWCA was founded and the first World Conference was held in Paris. By then it had long outgrown just the drapery trade, and the reputation of the association led to branches being established all over the world. In 1894 Queen Victoria knighted George Williams, and within ten years membership of the association had grown to well over 150,000. At the World YMCA Jubilee in 1905, although 84 and very infirm, he declared to the gathering, 'If you wish to have a happy, useful and profitable life, give your hearts to God while you are young.' He was then taken to his room, where he died shortly afterwards. He was buried in St. Paul's Cathedral and is celebrated in a stained glass window in Westminster Abbey.

Today the YMCA organisation lacks the evangelical impetus it had in its early days but continues to help in the physical and emotional development of youngsters across the world. The organisation now operates in over one hundred countries and can boast thirty million members, possibly the largest youth organisation in the world.

Sporting Greats

I have always felt a reluctance about using the word hero in respect of sportsmen and sportswomen. Are they really heroes when they are taking part in a sport or pastime which they love? Does it take bravery or courage? Read the sports pages of any national or local paper and an individual who is declared a hero one week can be dropped from the team the next. For me, sporting heroes are those who we can look back on and whose achievements still stand out. One such person is Mary Bignal Rand, Britain's first Olympic golden girl.

Another is cricket's greatest all rounder, Ian Botham, whose glory days are the years he played for Somerset. Botham's swashbuckling brilliance with bat and ball is far from forgotten, although we sometimes forget his long distance walks for charity, including his incredible walk over the Alps with Hannibal the elephant. Botham was also an accomplished footballer, a game which he played at league but not national level. But Botham would never lay claim to be the complete all rounder. Instead, consider a sportsman who played both cricket for England and rugby for England. And as if that was not enough, just for good measure also played hockey, billiards and even skittles for the county. And who also worked in a brewery.

Sammy Woods

Samuel Moses James Woods was not Somerset born and bred but it was the county he adopted. He was born in 1867 in Sydney, Australia, one of five sons, all of them athletic, with a larger number of sisters. His father was equally sporting and was reputed to be the strongest man to emigrate to Australia. At school, which necessitated a six mile each way river trip on a steamer, young Sammy excelled at cricket as both bowler and batsman. He also had a passion for rugby.

Early exposure to playing cricket 'overseas' came one Christmas when the family travelled to the island of Levuke, Fiji. There they were asked to play cricket against the native Fijians who won the toss and opted to bat. At the end of the first days play they were 175 for 72! Sammy had taken 25 of their wickets. It clearly wasn't being played with just eleven men on each side and young Sammy suspected that many of the Fijians went in to bat at least twice, 'they were so alike one couldn't tell t'other from which'.

Aged sixteen, Sammy Woods arrived in England, primarily for his education, and made Somerset his home when an opportunity arose to learn the brewing trade. He was sent to Brighton College where they played football, a game with which he was not impressed, albeit he was to play it at county level in later years. Cricket and rugby were his passion and he was to become a double blue at Cambridge during his time there between 1888 and 1891. In one game for the university he took all ten wickets, not as many as on Fiji but sufficient to ensure victory.

In 1886 the Australian cricket team were in England for a Test Series, but with a side depleted by injury. Sammy Woods was called upon to play for the country of his birth. The following year he played rugby for Somerset. On a tour of the north, he was playing against Lancashire, the favourites to win. Thanks in part to a fine drop goal from Sammy, Somerset triumphed and the Northern papers raised the question 'Where the 'ell is Somerset?' By 1889, Sammy had won his first international honours, playing rugby for England against Scotland in Edinburgh.

In 1893 he turned his hand to brewing, joining the Starkey, Knight and Ford Brewery Company at Wiveliscombe and at their Bridgwater premises in Northgate. In his reminiscences he wrote of beer, 'I always knew how to drink it, and still do . . . What a glorious two years, to be sure! Stag hunting, [rugby] football, cricket, skittles, etc. and we had a lovely pack of foot beagles, so you may imagine we all kept very fit.' What a contrast to the sportsmen of today.

Despite having played cricket in 1888 for Australia, he was invited to play for England in 1895 and 1896. He had already impressed the selectors with his performances for Somerset. In his first game for the county he took 12 wickets for 47 and continued to play for them from 1891 to 1910. At first class level he took 1040 wickets and scored 15,345 runs. In 1899 he was declared the 'Wisden Cricketer of the Year'.

Although unsubstantiated, I understand that there is one claim to fame which he preferred to forget. When W. G. Grace scored his hundredth century in first class cricket, the bowler was Sammy Woods. The players all left the field and a magnum of champagne was consumed. Play continued and Grace went on to hit 289.

He eventually retired in Bridgwater and died on 30 April 1931 at

Melville House Nursing Home in Taunton, where he was buried just inside the cemetery gates in St. Mary's Cemetery in Wellington Road, close to his beloved county cricket ground.

Mary Bignal Rand, MBE

Mary Bignal was born in February 1940 in the cathedral city of Wells and even as a girl made her mark as an athlete. Her potential became truly apparent when in the long jump in 1958 she jumped 5.84 metres in the Commonwealth Games, just missing the Commonwealth record. In the European Championships, still only eighteen, she set the first of her six British records at Pentathlon. The following year, she set eleven British records at long jump and new British records in the 100 metre sprint and 80 metre hurdles.

In 1960, the year she married fellow Olympian rower Sidney Rand, she entered the Olympic Games in Rome as the favourite for gold; but it was to be a disappointing games with ninth place being the best she could achieve. Ironically in the qualifying rounds she jumped 6.33 metres, which would have gained her a silver medal had she hit the same form in the finals. She missed the bronze in the hurdles by 0.1 seconds and her team dropped the baton in the relay. The games had been a personal disaster but in 1962, just four months after the birth of her daughter Alison, she took gold at long jump and bronze in the sprint relay in the European Games.

In the 1964 Tokyo Olympics she made up for her earlier disappointment when she triumphantly won the gold medal in convincing fashion, breaking three British and Olympic records and achieving a world record long jump of 6.76 metres. Four of her six jumps beat her personal best and the worst of them would still have been good enough to take silver.

At first she did not realise how far she had jumped. She was used to thinking in feet and inches, whilst Olympic measurements were metric. Had she known her jump was 22 feet, 2¼ inches, she would have savoured her victory that much sooner. What made it even more remarkable was that she jumped against a strong headwind and from an old style cinder track (the 1964 Olympics marked the last use of cinder in the long jump). In the same games she won a silver medal in the pentathlon setting a new British record, bronze in the sprint relay and came fourth in the hurdles.

Mary Bignal Rand had become the first British woman to achieve a track and field Olympic gold. It was an achievement which was to earn her the title of 'Sportswoman of the Year' and was followed by a well-deserved MBE in 1965.

No one was prouder of Mary Rand than the townspeople of Wells. In due course the city honoured her achievements in a more permanent fashion by recording the length of her jump in slabs of limestone set flush into the pavement in the market square. A bronze plaque marks one end, with the Olympic symbol of five rings at the other. It's only when one walks from one end to the other that one realises just how remarkable an athlete Mary Rand was.

Andy Elson – record breaking balloonist

Andy Elson lives in Masbury near Wells. Born in 1953, he spent his childhood in the village of Saltford between Keynsham and Bath. His adventurous spirit was revealed when he sailed his dinghy from the Devon coast to Cherbourg and back without telling his parents. The twenty hour trip was quite an adventure for a twelve year old.

His career began as an engineering apprentice before studying Aeronautical Engineering. Aged twenty three, he set up a design and manufacturing business. Within fourteen years the business had expanded and Andy had developed a passion for ballooning. After years of competing in ballooning events, he turned his engineering talents to the development of high altitude equipment

In August 1991 he flew in the world's first hot air balloon crossing of Mount Everest, the only time it has ever been achieved. He was lucky to survive. The flight was planned to cross a mountain peak on which would be a cameraman filming the balloonists. Andy allowed his balloon to descend to a lower level, to ensure the cameraman could get the required shots. He stayed too low, too long. Approaching Everest at 100 miles per hour, he had to turn on all five burners but then the load tapes, which hold the gondola to the balloon, began to melt. It was too late to parachute to safety. The burners had to be turned down. It was a narrow escape for the man who was to become the foremost designer and engineer of 'around the world balloons'.

The opportunity came to work on the Breitling sponsored Orbiter 1, for which Andy developed a suitable burner. During its flight, it had to ditch in the Mediterranean. Andy realised that the flight could have been successful had an engineer been on board, one like himself. By 1998 he had designed and built Breitling Orbiter 2 and was asked to be the third member of the crew in an attempt to fly around the world.

They set off from Switzerland and during the flight encountered a major problem. The gondola, suspended beneath the balloon, had two hatches, the lower of which served as an escape hatch and hence would fall away if opened. The seal of the lower hatch was leaking and had to be fixed before the balloon could ascend. At a height of 9,000 feet, and in a temperature of -7, Andy abseiled down the outside of the gondola, wearing an oxygen mask. He cleared away the offending grit and held the hatch in place while his fellow travellers clamped it into position. The gondola was safe to ascend to the high altitude jet stream. The flight ended in Burma, the Chinese authorities having refused permission to enter their airspace. But it had set a new world record for endurance flying of 9 days, 17 hours and 55 minutes.

The following year, in partnership with Colin Prescot, he flew from Spain to Japan on his Cable and Wireless flight, a journey which lasted 17 days, 18 hours and 25 minutes, shattering the earlier record. The journey ended when they ditched in the Pacific Ocean. Their achievement was recognised by the rarely awarded Royal Aero Club's Gold Medal, whose previous recipients include Bleriot, the Wright Brothers, Alcock and Brown, Aldrin and Collins, and Armstrong – giant names in the world of aviation.

In September 2003, Andy Elson and Colin Prescott failed in their attempt to shatter the world altitude record for a manned balloon flight. For two years they had waited for the opportunity to launch the balloon in which they planned to ascend to 132,000 feet, or 25 miles, and reach the very edge of space. Disaster struck when the 1,270 feet tall QinetiQ1 balloon suffered a tear and lay deflated on the launch pad. Fully inflated, it would have been taller than the Empire State Building with a surface area of nine acres. The weather's window of opportunity had passed for that year.

If space is the final frontier, Somerset can boast a truly heroic explorer in Andy Elson. Hopefully, in the near future, the world will hear of his successful attempt to break the altitude record on what he describes as 'a day trip to space'.

Index

Authers, Ron 61-66
Baker, Pte. N.W.S. 58-59
Banwell 45
Barkley, Frances 16, 19-23
Barrow, Bob 94-95
Batchelor, Douglas 87-88
Bath 27, 33, 35-38, 57-59, 70, 82, 102, 109
Batten-Pooll, Arthur Hugh Henry 50-51
Berrow 80
Biffen, Sarah 8-15
Blake, Edward 90
Blue Anchor 78
Bondfield, Margaret 16, 23-26
Botham, Ian 106
Braysdown Colliery 85-86
Bridges, Joseph 83
Bridgwater 10, 13, 16, 19, 27, 29, 33, 61, 66, 67, 70, 89-92, 104, 107
Brooks, Oliver 48-49
Brown, Dennis 91
Brown, Sgt. B 58
Browne, Captain George Lewis 67-70
Bruton 77
Buckland Dinham 44
Burnham-on-Sea 52-54, 56, 80-81, 96-97
Bythesea, Lt. John 70-71

Carter, James 83
Castle Cary 75
Chard 23, 26, 34, 39, 95-96, 100-102
Chard, Lt. John Rouse Merriott 40-44
Chewton Mendip 60
Clutterbuck, Lt. Daniel 27, 33
Cole, Henry 102-103
Collins, John 51
Combe St Nicholas 39
Congresbury 56, 98-99
Conygre Colliery 82-84
Cook, T J 60
Corton Denham 73
Crandon, Henry George 47
Crewkerne 45
Crimmin, John 39
Curtis, Denzil and Stan 94-95

Curtis, Stan 94-95

Dare, Grace (see Margaret Bondfield)
Davis, Captain J 79-80
Davis, David 96-97
Daw, Pte. Thomas 45
Day, Lt. George Fiott 71-72
Douglas, Campbell Mellis 72-73
Duke, Cpl. Frederick Alfred 59-60
Dulverton 104
Durham, James 83

East Quantoxhead 8, 12, 14
Elson, Andy 109-110
Elton, Major Frederick Cockayne 34
Escott, Captain 79-80
Exford 87-88
Exmoor 87-89, 94-95

Fear, John 83
Foley, Francis 51-56
Fosbery, Lt. George Vincent 38-39
Fowler, George 83
Freshford 70
Fricker, Enoch 83-84
Frome 17, 44, 48, 50, 90
Fuller, Wilfred Dolby 48

Gage, John 83
Gillingham, James 100
Glastonbury 27, 29-30, 33
Golledge, Herbert 85-86
Grice, George 83-84
Griffiths, Thomas 90-91

Harding, George 83
Hardwick, Charles Capell 98-99
Hatch Beauchamp 40
Henson, William 101
Heron, Denis 27-34
Highbridge 51-52
Howse, Sir Neville Reginald 46
Hussey, Lawrence 95-96
Hutton 96

James, Eric 95-96
Jerome, Captain Henry Edward 37
Jones, John 90

Keeling, John 83
Keynsham 109
Kilton 13
Kilve 13
Knight, Henry James 46-47

Langport 90
Larkbarrow 88
Le Patourel, Herbert Wallace 60-61
Leslie, Sgt-Mjr J. A. 58-59

Maillard, William Job 45-46
Martell, Pte. J.M. 58-59
Masbury 109
Meadowcroft, Ken 91
Mellish, Reverend Edward Noel 49-50
Merriott 45
Midsomer Norton 48
Minehead 79
Mullins, Special Constable Frank 88

Nicholas, A. and Simon 79-80
Norton FitzWarren 92
Odcombe 35
Orchard, Pte. George Edward 44
Otterhampton 19

Paulton 44
Pearce, Alfred 96
Pitcombe 77
Pitman, Herbert John 75-77
Place, Basil Godfrey 73
Pollard, H J 60
Porlock Weir 60
Prescott, Colin 110
Press, Coxswain Henry 78

Quantock Hills 9
Rand, Mary Bignal 106, 108-109
Reade, Herbert Taylor 36
Rees, Pte. H D 58-59
Reeves, Andrew, Ruth and James 96-97
Renny, Lt.George Alexander 36-37
Reynolds, Lt. 56
Ridler, J 60

Rogers, Mary Ann 17-19
Roope, Gerard Broadmead 73-75

Saltford 109
Saxty, Cpl Alfred 44
Seaman, Joseph 91
Short, Tom 83-84
Shoscombe 86
Simonsbath 87-88, 94-95
South Petherton 49-50, 90
Sperring, George 83
Steart 80
Stogursey 46
Stringfellow, John 101-102
Strong, George 34-35
Stubbles, Paul 92-94
Sutton Montis 75

Talbot, Fanny 16-17
Taunton 40, 48, 73, 92, 108
Timsbury 82-85
Trott, PC 88
Vickery, Samuel 39-40
Vigars, Frank 87-88

Waller, Col. William Francis Frederick 37-38
Watchet 78-80
Webb, Cpl. E.E. 57-58
Wedlake, Alfred 79-80
Weeks, George 85-86
Wellington 45
Wellow 85-86
Wells 39, 47, 72, 90, 108-109
West Hatch 51
Weston-super-Mare 71-72, 81
Whitestaunton 34
Wilcox, Edward 27, 29-30, 33
Williams, George 104-105
Williams, Paul 92-94
Wines, George 90
Withypool 87
Wiveliscombe 107
Woods, Sammy 106-108
Woolavington 96
Woolmer, Mrs. J.M. 57
Woolverton 50
Yeovil 34, 46, 56, 90
Yeovilton 59